THE
SAMSON
AND
DELILAH
COMPLEX

THE SAMSON AND DELILAH COMPLEX

Keep Your Independence Without Losing Your Lover

Eva Margolies

Louis Genevie, Ph. D.

Dodd, Mead & Company

NEW YORK

THIS BOOK IS DEDICATED TO
OUR CHILDREN, DAVID AND MELISSA,
that they may live in a world
free of fear

No part of this book may be reproduced in any form
without permission in writing from the publisher.
Published by Dodd, Mead & Company, Inc.
79 Madison Avenue, New York, N.Y. 10016
Distributed in Canada by
McClelland and Stewart Limited, Toronto

Manufactured in the United States of America

Designed by Claire Counihan

First Edition

1   2   3   4   5   6   7   8   9   10

Library of Congress Cataloging-in-Publication Data

Margolies, Eva.
The Samson and Delilah complex.

Bibliography: p.
Includes index.
1. Men—Psychology.   2. Dominance (Psychology)
3. Fear.   4. Sex role.   I. Genevie, Louis E.
II. Title.
HQ1090.M37   1986   305.3   86-6331
ISBN 0-396-08792-2

Contents

Acknowledgments

There are many people who helped make this book better than we could have done alone. For her psychological insights, we owe our gratitude to Angela Fox, who is a psychoanalyst in private practice in New York City. Patricia Brown, a therapist in Vermont, also shed light on the nature of male-female relationships. Our in-house editor, Patricia Quilliam, paid patient attention to detail and was extremely helpful in the development of the original manuscript. We would also like to thank Jerry Gross, our editor at Dodd, Mead, who helped shape the direction of this book and whose editorial skill was pivotal in putting together the final draft of this volume. Dr. June Kallos kindly read and commented on the manuscript, and Ruth Margolies spent many hours discussing her ideas and sharing her experiences with us. We are also grateful to our teenage children, David and Melissa, who patiently listened as we discussed the ideas that went into this book and who offered relevant anecdotes about the Samsons and Delilahs among their own generation. Finally, we are indebted to the many men and women who shared their stories with us. Without them, this book could not have been written.

Prologue:
The Story of
Samson and Delilah

In biblical times, a man named Samson, who was endowed with great physical strength, fell in love with a Philistine priestess named Delilah. The Philistine leaders viewed Samson as an enemy because he refused to submit to their rule. They approached Delilah and promised to pay her eleven hundred pieces of silver if she would entice Samson into confessing the source of his great strength to her. Delilah's allegiance to her people was greater than her love for Samson, and so she agreed.

"Please tell me wherein your great strength lies, and how you might be bound, that one could subdue you," she implored Samson. To which her lover responded, "If they bind me with seven fresh bowstrings that have not been dried, then I shall become weak, and be like any other man." Delilah bound Samson with the bowstrings, but when the Philistines came upon him, he broke the bowstrings with ease.

Delilah tried wheedling his secret out of him once again. "Behold, you have mocked me, and told me lies; please tell me how you might be bound." And Samson told her, "If they bind me with new ropes that have not been used, then I shall become weak, and be like any other man." Once again, Delilah bound him. And once again, when the Philistines came upon Samson, he snapped the ropes off his arms as though they were threads.

Delilah then approached Samson for a third time. "Until now you have mocked me, and told me lies; tell me how you might be bound." Once again, Samson gave his mistress a phony story. "If you weave the seven locks of my head with the web and make it tight with the pin, then I shall become weak, and be like any other man." When Samson was asleep, Delilah did just that. But when the Philistines came to seize him, he pulled away the pin, the loom, and the web.

Delilah was becoming increasingly frustrated. "How can you say 'I love you' when your heart is not with me? You have mocked me these three times, and you have not told me wherein your great strength lies." Day after day, she pressed him hard until Samson's soul "was vexed to death." Finally, he told her the secret. "A razor has never come upon my head. . . . If I be shaved, then my strength will leave me, and I shall become weak, and be like any other man." Delilah then made Samson sleep in her lap, and when he was sound asleep, she called a man who shaved off Samson's hair. Upon awakening, Samson was still convinced that he possessed his strength. It was not until the Philistines came upon him that he realized that his strength had left him. The Philistines gouged out Samson's eyes and bound him with bronze fetters.

After a time, the Philistines brought Samson from his prison cell to publicly humiliate him. Bringing him to the great temple, they had him stand between the pillars on which the great house rested. The arena was packed to see the spectacle of the fallen superman. But Samson prayed to the Lord to give him back his strength just for a moment, and the Lord complied. Samson grasped the pillars, leaned his weight on them, and pushed them apart. The pillars collapsed, and the great temple crumbled and fell upon the crowd. The Philistines, including Delilah, were killed, and Samson, the man of strength, went down with them.

Introduction

This is a book about men who fear women, how they get to be that way, and what women can do to help them overcome their fear.

Men have always had some fear of women, just as women have always had some fear of men. Distrust between the sexes has always existed because of the lack of familiarity of each sex with the other. But for a large number of men, their fear of women is so pervasive that it threatens to destroy (and in some cases has destroyed) their relationships with the women they love. The fear shows itself in an ever-present need to keep women down, to control them economically or emotionally. We call a man who experiences this degree of fear a Samson because, as we shall shortly see, Samson had a dire fear of women, which he hid behind a facade of superior strength.

In fact, we discovered an often-predictable pattern of increasingly strong defenses used by a man to keep the woman in his life under his thumb, thereby keeping his fear hidden. We call the relationship between a Samson and the woman in his life *the Samson and Delilah Complex*, because the more a man tries to stand in the way of a woman's growth and development, the more likely a woman will behave like the abandoning, belittling, betraying Delilah that he so fears.

Although the strong fear that some men have of women is not new, it has become more difficult to hide. As women become increasingly able to fend for themselves financially, the primary source of men's ability to control women is being taken away. Contrary to the belief that most men are becoming more liberated, there is every reason to believe that many men's fear of women is getting worse.

Over the years, we have observed the Samson and Delilah Complex as therapists and sociologists. We have seen it in patients, colleagues, and friends. We have heard about it from other mental health professionals, as well as from the women—and occasionally men—whom we interviewed. Invariably, the pattern has been the same: the more a woman came into her own and felt good about her growth and development, the more threatened and controlling the man in her life became. A Samson who used his economic superiority as the primary way of keeping a woman tied to him, for example, often became overly possessive or withdrawing when the woman in his life became economically self-sufficient. When those defenses failed to control her or in cases when a man's fear was particularly strong, he became humiliating, sabotaging, and sometimes even physically violent. When none of these controls worked, or when the woman in his life threatened to or actually did leave him, he began to fall apart. Indeed, we observed that this pattern of using increasingly strong controls was the hallmark of a Samson, the trait that sets him apart from his non-Samson counterpart.

Except in cases where a man was so threatened by his mate's new assertiveness that he left first, we also noticed a predictable response on the part of women living with Samsons. Some women became so angry and frustrated by what they viewed as chauvinistic domination that they left the relationship. In other instances, the woman submitted to her man's control and remained in the relationship physically, but she pulled away emotionally. In both cases, the anger and resentment of these women ran deep.

While most men have a little Samson in them, not all men are Samsons. By the time you finish reading Chapter 3, you'll have a good idea of whether or not the man in your life is a Samson and how much of a Samson he is. The one exception is the "closet" Samson, that is, the man whose fear has not shown itself because the woman in his life chooses to submit to his control.

This is an important point. Although a woman is usually not

responsible for creating a Samson (that is, unless she is the kind of Delilah we discuss in Chapter 9), women often have the choice of giving in to a Samson's fear or challenging it and helping him free himself from it. That is why this book is largely directed to women who have a close relationship with a Samson. Although you may not be the direct cause of his fear, you are probably the best person to help him get past it. Part II of this volume is devoted to explaining just how you can do that. Chapter 13 is specifically written for men who are motivated enough to overcome their fear on their own.

Our findings are based on several years of professionally observing and, in Eva Margolies's case, counseling, men and women; on hundreds of books and articles from professional journals, newspapers, and magazines; and on over one hundred interviews with men and women from varying backgrounds between the ages of twenty and sixty that were conducted expressly for this book. The stories on the following pages are true, but all identifying characteristics have been changed to protect the identity of those to whom we spoke.

We have tried to bring to this book a viewpoint that is neither male nor female but a combination of both. In the past, books about the relationship between the sexes have usually been slanted to the sex of the individual author. We spent many hours merging our thoughts and ideas so that we could avoid such a bias.

Most important, our goal is to be helpful. We believe that most men are good people who have strengths and weaknesses. Our intent is not to deride men but to help women understand men better and to help men understand themselves.

In this book, you will meet men you have loved and stopped loving; men you want to love but are having trouble loving; men you love but often hate. You will point your finger at these men and probably say, "These are not Samsons, these are chauvinists!" But we ask you not to take their machismo, their chauvinism at face value. For behind every sexist, behind every closet chauvinist, there is a man who is terribly afraid; a man who wants to be loved but whose fear stands in the way; a man who needs your help if he is ever to overcome his fear.

PART I

SAMSON AND HIS FEARS

Chapter 1
Men's Hidden Fear

He's an absolute pushover when it comes to a beautiful woman, completely unable to contain his passion. He's utterly dependent emotionally on the woman in his life. He feels insecure about his manhood. And he is terribly afraid of women.

Do you recognize this man? No, he is not a wimp. Nor is he your classic loser. Neither is he a mama's boy. The man described above is the biblical Samson.

When most of us think of Samson, a completely different image comes to mind: strong, powerful, in control, a leader of men who was betrayed by the shrewd Delilah. But have you ever stopped to consider why Samson got involved with Delilah in the first place? Sure, she was beautiful, but he knew that she was dangerous from the start. What made him confess the secret of his great strength to Delilah even though he knew his life was at stake? After all, she did not hold a gun to his head. With all of Samson's strength, how could he have been reduced to the stature of a prisoner by a woman who knew his greatest weakness?

A close reading of the Samson and Delilah story reveals the real reason for Samson's downfall. As much as he exuded strength and confidence, when it came to Delilah, he was insecure and vulnerable. His sexual urges overran his ability to think clearly. Emotionally, he needed Delilah a lot more than she needed him, and he was terrified of being rejected by her—a fear that led him to confess the secret of his strength and that ultimately led to his downfall. For all his supposed superiority, Samson's great strength was highly precarious. His best-guarded secret was not that his power resided in his hair but that Delilah had tremendous power over him—power that he greatly feared.

How many men today come across as being superior to women but deep down harbor a tremendous fear of them? In our research, we found men's fear of women to be pervasive, cutting across class and ethnic boundaries. He may be the corporate president who pays lip service to equality for women but who does not allow his wife to work, or he may be the working-class man who insists that women are inferior to men. He may be your spouse, your lover, your friend, even your son. Whoever he is, his veneer of strength and superiority to women can be convincing.

At first glance, you would not think that he is vulnerable or his strength fallible. But have you ever wondered why he is so threatened by the idea of a woman making as much money as he? If he is so secure in his manhood, why does he need to prove how superior he is again and again? Why does he have to put women down or act as if he doesn't need them much at all? The answer is that like Samson, he, too, harbors a deep and hidden fear of women that arises out of his vulnerability to them and his own precarious masculinity. He, too, is terrified that his secret fear will be discovered, a fear that he hides by trying to keep women under his thumb. His unconscious rationale is that if he does not control the woman in his life, he will be controlled *by* her.

What makes the modern-day Samson different from his biblical counterpart is that Samson was unable to control Delilah—she was independently wealthy, for one thing, thereby denying Samson the economic superiority through which today's Samson exerts much of his power. But the more today's Samson loses his economic control, the more like the ancient Samson he becomes—needy, vulnerable, frightened. And the more frightened he becomes, the greater is his need to control the woman that he fears.

Herein lies the great tragedy. Just as Samson was an enemy of the Philistines (and hence of Delilah) because he used his strength to control them, the modern-day Samson makes enemies of the women he tries to control. What results, in both cases, is a desire on her part to flee or seek revenge. In essence, men's fear of women and their resulting need to control women gives rise to the abandoning, betraying woman that men fear most: Delilah.

The Myth of the Dangerous Woman

Although there has been very little written about it, men's fear of women is not new. What has been written about the subject places the blame for men's fear of women on women themselves by portraying them as innately manipulative and castrating. Almost universally, women have been portrayed both as goddesses who build a man's ego and as villainesses who diminish a man's eminence and sap his strength. Beginning in the Garden of Eden, when Eve enticed Adam to eat the forbidden fruit, and continuing to the medieval Church, which considered women "a necessary evil, a natural temptation, a desirable calamity, a domestic peril, a deadly fascination, a painted ill,"[1] men have blamed their fear of women on women's evil nature. "It is not that I dread women," the collective sentiment seems to be, "but that women are innately dangerous."

Nor are the sentiments expressed in these stories relics from ancient times. Modern-day versions of the "castrating woman" story crop up frequently on television and in the movies. One riveting example is the 1981 film *Body Heat,* starring William Hurt and Kathleen Turner. Hurt portrays a weak-willed lawyer who becomes besotted by Turner, the stunning, seductive wife of a prominent businessman. He is awed to find that his passion for her is reciprocated. According to Turner, only one thing prevents their relationship from being perfect: her husband. During the course of their torrid affair, Turner insidiously hints that if her husband were out of the way, she and Hurt could be together always. Blinded by his infatuation with her and the thought of possessing her completely, Hurt agrees to carry out her plot to murder her husband.

The scheming vixen has other plans for Hurt, however. The murder successfully committed, Turner sets in motion an elaborate chain of events that makes it appear that she has died in a fire. She adopts a new identity and disappears, leaving him to take the blame not only for her husband's murder but also for her own.

Whether ancient or modern, the message is clear: for a man, to get involved with a woman is to write the script for his destruction.

Indeed, if we were asked to summarize the moral of these stories, it would sound something like this: "Women are by nature manipulative, castrating bitches; dangerous villainesses who are not to be trusted and who must be controlled. If men are afraid of women, it is because women give men every reason to fear them."

While this is partly true, it is not the complete picture. The Samson and Delilah story and the pervasive myth of the castrating woman suggest a different reality. Men may blame women for their own fear of them, but it is men's own vulnerability, not women's dangerous nature, that men fear most. In our research, we identified three vulnerabilities that give rise to men's fears:

· Men are more preoccupied with women sexually than women are with men, leading to men's fear of being sexually controlled by women.

· For psychological and social reasons, men need women emotionally more than women need men. This results in a fear of being emotionally controlled, abandoned, or completely dependent.

· Because men are raised by women, coupled with the fact that men cannot bear children, many men feel uncertain of their masculinity. As a result, many men are motivated to dominate women and prove their superiority to them as a way of asserting their maleness. At the same time, men fear that they are inferior to women in many ways, and they are terrified that if women discover their secret, their masculinity will be destroyed.

In a moment, we will return to the Samson and Delilah story and trace the origins of men's hidden fear. But before going on, it is important to say that women are afraid of men, too. Like men, most women experience the fear of being abandoned and the fear of being controlled. Women, too, often fear that they are inferior. But the fear that many men have of women goes much deeper and is more profound, for men's fear has its origin in certain biological, psychological, and socially immutable facts. That first unchangeable "fact" is male physiology itself.

The Fear of Sexual Control

When most people think about the downfall of the biblical Samson, the image that comes to mind is that of a poor soul who just happened to get involved with the wrong kind of woman. Our inclination is to feel sorry for him because Delilah duped him into believing that she was as much in love with him as he was with her.

But a closer examination of Samson and Delilah's relationship reveals that contrary to popular belief, Samson was well aware of Delilah's intention to betray him. In fact, Samson was no unknowing, innocent victim of Delilah's seduction at all, but rather he was the victim of his own insatiable libido.

You need look no further than the first act of Saint-Saëns's 1877 operative version, *Samson et Dalila*, to discover the real source of Samson's decline. Samson is resting in a garden when a group of dancing girls comes along, one of whom is Delilah. Samson takes one look at her and desires her. At this point, one of Samson's aides tells him plainly that becoming involved with Delilah is like playing with fire.

What does Samson do with this information? He ignores it. He also ignores his own gut impulse that tells him that falling in love with Delilah will lead to nothing but trouble:

> *Cover her features, whose beauty*
> *disturbs my senses, troubles my soul.*
> *Extinguish the fire of her eyes*
> *that robs me of my liberty.*[2]

The biblical version of Samson and Delilah's relationship is even more revealing. Samson falls in love with Delilah, who had been enlisted by the Philistines to prod the secret of his strength from him. At an opportune moment, she implores Samson to share his secret with her. Samson, who is rightly suspicious of his lover, makes up a lie: he tells her that if he were bound with seven fresh bowstrings that have not been dried, then he would become as weak as any other mortal. Believing his story, Delilah betrays him. She has the Philistines bring her the bowstrings, and she binds Samson with them when he is asleep. Of course, it doesn't take Delilah long to figure out that Samson has deceived her. As soon as the Philistines come to take him prisoner, Samson snaps the bowstrings with no effort at all.

Now here's the extraordinary part. Even though Samson's hunch that Delilah is not to be trusted, that she is out to destroy him, has been confirmed, he still cannot resist her. Two more times, Delilah asks him to divulge the secret of his strength; two more times, he gives her a phony answer. And two more times, Delilah betrays him. Still he keeps going back for more, and on the fourth go-around, he tells her his secret.

Is the message of all of this that Samson was a masochist? No, just the opposite. Samson was a man driven by an uncontrollable need for sex. He was not some poor unknowing victim but a man who could not control his lustful impulses, his own libido. Samson may have been the strongest man on earth, but for all his supposed physical prowess, he was putty when confronted with Delilah's sexual temptation. He was a man who was capable of knocking down fortresses, but he felt that Delilah had the power to rob him of his liberty by sexually controlling him. Delilah did have power over him—power wrought out of Samson's own weakness: his vulnerability to Delilah's sexual allure—which was why he feared her so, why she "troubled his soul."

Many men today share this dread of being sexually controlled by women.[3] In real life, the man who submits to a woman is in little danger of having his hair or his genitalia cut off. But he is never without the unconscious feeling that he is at the mercy of his own sexuality and hence at *her* mercy. The fear is so pervasive that many anthropologists believe that it is almost universal.[4]

The fear of being sexually controlled by women shows up symbolically in men's dread of the vagina. Many cultures have a myth referred to as the *vagina dentata*—according to which, women's vaginas are equipped with sharp, biting teeth. Men's dread of the vagina is no stranger to psychoanalysts like Karen Horney, who see it appearing time and again among their patients, usually in the form of dreams about being swallowed up or falling into a bottomless crevice or pit.[5]

The source of this anxiety, as the Samson and Delilah story suggests, is that men are more preoccupied with sex than women, but women control sexual access. That is not to say that women do not have a need for sex; indeed, their capacity for orgasm is greater. But there is little doubt that men's obsession with and need for sex are generally stronger. Studies show that men think about sex a lot more than women do. The average man has thoughts about sex six times an hour on the average. Even in his forties, when his sexual capacity begins to wane, erotic thoughts still cross his mind once an hour or so. Men also dream about sex more than women do—three times more—dreams that are filled with fantasy Venuses whom they are seducing. A man's sexual fantasy life is also a lot more torrid and active than a woman's. Although women day-dream about love, romance, and sometimes sex, for men it's sex, sex, sex all the way.[6]

This obsessional preoccupation with sex comes, in large part, from biology. As animal studies suggest, the sex drive among the male of the species is usually stronger than that of the female. The powerful male libido also has a strong psychological component. For men, the ability to conquer a woman with his "weapon" is a symbol of power, and masculinity is largely based on how much power a man thinks he has. For some men, the tremendous need for intercourse may also be a cover-up for an unexpressed need for love and closeness, for that complete and utter feeling of fusion that the boy had with his mother when he was little.[7]

Whatever the source, a man's often obsessional preoccupation with sex leaves him in the vulnerable position of being controlled. He wants it; she's got it. He has to ask for it, but she can refuse it. At the very least, she dictates the conditions under which she will give it to him. Simply put, he is at her mercy.

A few men have some awareness of this vulnerability. "I've got-ten involved with a number of women who have used sex as a kind of reward," one man told us. "It's a type of one-upmanship—'If you're nice, maybe I will. If you're not, maybe I won't.' I hate that, and as soon as I think that's the way a woman is operating, my impulse is to stay clear of her. But when a woman is really attractive, I just can't seem to help myself. So I end up getting mad at myself for being 'led around by the balls,' as they say, and I end up resenting the woman for doing that to me."

Adding insult to injury is the fact that the adult male's predica-ment is a replication of his experience in the early mother-son re-lationship. The first person that a boy depends on is his mother. From the beginning, he has to obtain nourishment and satisfaction from her, yet he is vulnerable and she is powerful. Now, as an adult, he once again has to struggle to gain access to a woman. In the face of his pressing libido, he is again at a woman's mercy, for once again she can always cut off access. Throughout his life, he continues to be reminded of a woman's power and of his own powerlessness.

Added to all this is the fact that at the end of the sexual act, men are left physically depleted and weak. "Each time a man has sex, he loses power," psychoanalyst Angela Fox told us. "He starts out in a physically strong way with an erect penis, but he ends up with a completely useless, impotent object. He feels depleted; he feels his strength sapped. Consciously, he feels exhausted and deeply satisfied. Unconsciously, however, he feels castrated. Can you imagine a man trying to defend the world after an orgasm?" This, Ms. Fox told us, leaves the male in a dilemma. "He's lured by something that will give him satisfaction and a feeling of power, but at the same time he also must witness his own weakness."

Although it is powerful in and of itself, men's fear of being controlled sexually by women is just the tip of the iceberg. Even more compelling is their fear of being abandoned by them. A brief return to the Samson and Delilah story will demonstrate just how deep that fear goes.

The Weakness—Dependence; The Fear— Emotional Abandonment

Although it is true that Samson's insatiable libido got him into Delilah's bed, it was Delilah's emotional hold over him, not her sexual hold, that really got him into trouble. In fact, Samson confided his secret to her *not* at a moment of high passion, but when Delilah accused him of not loving her, *when she was threatening to leave him!* As the operatic version of the story goes, Delilah tries unsuccessfully to get Samson to tell her the source of his great strength. She begs, she pleads, all to no avail. But when she tells Samson she is going to leave him, he has a sudden change of heart. "Coward, unloving heart!" accuses Delilah. "I despise you. Farewell."[8] At that point, Samson breaks down and tells her all.

The real truth about Samson is this: he may have been able to fight off armies by himself, but the thought of losing his beloved Delilah's love was something he simply could not cope with. Delilah's sexual power over him made Samson vulnerable, but it was his profound *emotional* dependence, his terrifying fear of being abandoned by her, that ultimately destroyed him.

How many men are there who, like Samson, appear to be strong and in control on the outside but who are emotionally vulnerable on the inside, who are so emotionally dependent on women that the idea of rejection pushes them to the brink of insanity? The research evidence on men, women, and love provides a clue. One study found that men, not women, are the incurable romantics. They fall in love much faster than women do, and they fall in love more often.[9] Women, on the other hand, are much more pragmatic about love, thinking less about love per se than about a man's economic prospects.[10]

If men fall in love more quickly, they also fall apart more devastatingly when love is lost. They become deeply depressed and unbearably lonely. Their whole mental frame of mind suffers. "When we compare . . . divorced men with divorced women, and widowed men with widowed women," a compilation of studies on the divorced and widowed concludes, "in each case it is men who are much more likely to be residents of mental hospitals."[11] And consider that the death rate of divorced men exceeds the death rate of divorced women by *three hundred percent!*[12] For many men, abandonment by a woman is not only an augury of poor mental health; it can be life-threatening as well.

You might now be thinking, "What about those fancy-free, swinging bachelors who hail the singles life as part of the American Dream?" That's the image that they want to project, and there are likely some men who truly do feel this way. But most swinging bachelors are, in actuality, down in the dumps compared with those poor "old maids" that we've come to pity. Single men have a higher rate of mental health problems than single women.[13] And the suicide rate for bachelors may be up to four times as high as the rate for their female counterparts![14]

All told, a man who is abandoned by a woman in his life, or who does not have a woman in his life, is significantly more at risk of mental and physical ailments and of death than a woman in a similar situation.

What we find in research, we also hear in popular songs time and time again. Listen to pop radio, and you'll discover that more often than not, it is men who are crooning the melancholy of love lost—a rather desperate crooning at that, if one really listens to the lyrics. In his song "I Can't Live Without You," Barry Manilow tells us that without his love he can't smile or sing; in fact, he can't seem to do much of anything.

And what are the women singing? Well, there's Cyndi Lauper telling us that "Girls Just Want to Have Fun" and Madonna admitting straight out that she's a "Material Girl"—a far cry from the overly sentimental romantics that women have been purported to be. Even in the throes of rejection, the hurt that women sing about does not have the same searing quality of rejection. While Manilow is having difficulty going on with his life, Gloria Gaynor is telling us in no uncertain terms, "I Will Survive, I Will Survive." And Tina Turner is asking, "What's Love Got to Do with It?"

We're certainly not saying that all we've heard about women needing men is a fantasy. While women need and want to be with men, the truth is that they aren't nearly as dependent on men emotionally as men are on women. As anthropologist Ashley Montagu put it, women just don't need men as "basically, pressingly, as men need women."[15]

You may be wondering, "How can this be?" The answer is relatively simple. From birth through boyhood, a boy is deeply dependent on his mother. She is both his first love and his lifeline. If she doesn't feed him, he doesn't eat; if she doesn't nurture him, he feels unloved; if she doesn't tend to him, he does not survive. Although a boy eventually gives up his attachment to his mother, he still continues to view other women as his lifeline, "his connection to survival, his energy source."[16]

Women, on the other hand, never develop the same kind of profound dependence on the male. The male was never responsible for her emotional survival; he was never her lifeline. It's her mother that a girl depends on for her emotional and physical well-being, not her father. On the contrary, a girl, like a boy, views her dad as more distant than her mother.[17] She may love him, even idolize him in the way that only a daughter can, but she never depends on him the way she depends on her mom. Not surprisingly, as an adult, although a woman may want an intimate relationship with a man, she can adapt more readily without one.[18] She has already learned to deal with a somewhat distant relationship with her father as a child. For the same reason, should she be abandoned or rejected by a man, the trauma, although painful, isn't nearly as devastating.

But this is only part of the explanation. While a little girl is learning that it's all right to express her feelings and to develop close ties with many people, particularly other women, a little boy is learning to cauterize his emotions in the name of breaking away from his mother and becoming a "man." And because it is not manly to express need and vulnerability, particularly to another male, a severe damper is placed on boys' ability to be intimate with each other. This incapacity to be close to other males specifically, and to form intimate bonds generally, leaves men at a distinct emotional disadvantage compared with women. A woman may want and love men, but when it comes right down to it, she can do without them. There are others in her life that she can count on for emotional intimacy.

And what about a man? Unless he is one of the few who are lucky enough to break free of the societal dictates that cripple him emotionally, he is left in a vulnerable position indeed. He is so vulnerable that Herb Goldberg, a leading psychologist in the area of male development, believes that this is one of the main reasons that women in our culture live so much longer than men. "I believe that unconsciously the male is afraid that he cannot survive without the woman," he writes in *The Hazards of Being Male*. "Outside of his strong attachment to his woman, he is often an isolated, alienated being. He has few close male friends. He has suppressed his interest in other women and has been a passive, noninvolved father to his children. All his needs are invested in her." He goes on to say that after a woman loses a man, however, "she still has close relationships to nourish her, other women and her children. Being less dependent on the male, she can make it with or without a man." [19]

"After I broke up with my girlfriend of two years, I was really a basket case," confessed Charles Jameson, a twenty-nine-year-old stockbroker. "But after a week or so of being very distraught [he kept in touch with her for a few months after the breakup], my girlfriend seemed to snap out of it. I couldn't understand it until one day I saw her with two of her friends, laughing and giggling and having a great time. Then it dawned on me: she had other people who were close to her to share her troubles, to spend time with. Me? I was all alone."

What adds fuel to men's anxiety about abandonment is that deep down they suspect that they are unable to provide women with the kind of emotional nourishment that women need. That's because women, like men, want nurturing, and men are not raised to be nurturers. On the contrary, many men tend to suppress their nurturant feelings so as to present a more masculine image. The result is that women often feel emotionally deprived in their relationships with men, eventually turning to others, particularly to other women, for the emotional nourishment that they need.[20]

This leaves men in a double bind: men need women emotionally more than women need men, but men often cannot give women what they need emotionally—which, of course, leaves men that much more vulnerable to being rejected. Margaret Mead summed the situation up perfectly: "Men have always been afraid that women could do without them."[21]

Given all this, it's no surprise that men are so fearful about not being needed by women and about being abandoned by them. Nor is it surprising that women's increasing economic self-sufficiency has given men's fear an additional edge. On some level, many men feel that women marry out of economic need as much as, if not more than, out of love. It is not a big jump for them to believe that if women become economically independent, they will no longer need men.

This leads us to men's greatest false assumption: their belief in their superiority over women.

The Fear—Inferiority

"I am nothing but an object of derision."
—SAMSON,
after his hair has been cut off[22]

For a man who was supposedly the epitome of masculinity, Samson was certainly sexually and emotionally vulnerable to Delilah. His great strength was limited to his physical prowess.

The irony is that, as limited as Samson's strength was, it was nevertheless the cornerstone of his masculinity. His conception of maleness was tied up with his superior physical prowess—a real problem when you consider how iffy that prowess truly was. It's understandable that Samson's greatest fear was that if Delilah discovered the source of his strength, she would have the power to emasculate him. When the foundation is so unsure, it doesn't take much to blow the building down.

Today's man is much like the biblical Samson. He, too, bases the whole of his masculinity on his greater strength—specifically, his economic and social superiority. It is through this superiority that men have been able to hide their sexual and emotional vulnerability to women. Intuiting that they cannot control their driving sexual need or their profound dependence on women, men have tried to control women by making them economically dependent on men.

But as was Samson's, men's strength is fallible, particularly today as women are becoming more economically self-sufficient. As men's hidden weakness is being uncovered, the whole of their masculinity is being shaken. When men are stripped of their economic and social superiority, what is revealed is a mortal who is not superior to women at all. If anything, men are, in many ways, inferior to women.

The Myth of the Weaker Sex

"Women are the weaker sex."

"Women are slaves to their emotions."

"Women are fragile and delicate. Put them in a tough situation, and they fall apart."

So we have been told, and so many women have come to believe. (We'll see later that this belief is at the root of much of what men view as Delilah-like behavior.) But all of the above statements are, quite simply, pure rubbish. In fact, notions about men being the superior sex are so erroneous that the arguments against them could fill a book—and did. In his groundbreaking volume *The Natural Superiority of Women,* anthropologist Ashley Montagu tore down the almighty-male, weak-and-helpless female doctrine bit by compelling bit.

First, let's look at the idea that women are the weaker sex. It *is* true that men are, on the average, physically stronger and larger than women. But their superiority, biologically speaking, starts and ends there. From the womb on, it is the male of the species that is more physically vulnerable than the female! More male than female fetuses are aborted spontaneously. And although five percent more males than females are born each year, by the time men and women are in their teens, that five percent advantage has disappeared. From then on, it's downhill for the male; males die eight years earlier than females on the average.[23]

Many people believe that the gap in life expectancy between men and women has been closing. After all, until recently, women have largely been protected from the stresses and pressures of the outside world. As more and more women go to work, we might expect that they, too, would start dying younger. But this has not been the case. In 1920, when the majority of women were being economically supported, the life expectancy for women was only one year higher than for men. Today, it is eight years higher, added stress and all. The disparity is so great that one study done at Harvard University predicted that at the rate we're going, by the year 2000 there will be 100 men for every 145 women![24]

The reason for this tremendous difference is largely genetic. Women's extra X chromosome not only determines sex but also carries genes that guard against infection.[25] Not surprisingly, women are also far more resistant to disease than men. More men than women die from heart disease, cancer, cerebrovascular disease, influenza, pneumonia, and arteriosclerosis, to name a few.[26] Even when women are more susceptible to a disease, as is the case with high blood pressure, more men die from it.[27]

It is true that as women have assumed the role of breadwinner and all the stress associated with that role, the incidence of ulcers, heart disease, and lung cancer among women has risen. While the gap in susceptibility to disease between men and women has been reduced, it still exists. The fact remains that women cope with stress better than men.

Men may accuse women of being led around by their emotions, continuously on emotional tenterhooks, but when it comes to dealing with the trials and tribulations of living, women are the real survivors. According to Montagu, not only do women handle stress of the everyday variety better than men, but they also endure pain and disaster as well as "all sorts of devitalizing conditions better than men: starvation, exposure, fatigue, shock, illness and the like."[28] So much for the notion that women are physically and emotionally more fragile than men.

Women may also have greater intellectual capabilities in certain areas. Throughout life, for example, females consistently excel in linguistic skills such as reading and speaking. Their memories are sharper. They have more vivid imaginations. It is also true that women, if not more intelligent, are better test takers than men. When a comparative study of intelligence test scores between girls and boys was conducted, a definitive conclusion was reached: with the exception of tests for arithmetic, mechanics, and mazes, "females achieve significantly and consistently higher scores on intelligence than males."[29]

Added to all this is the fact that women have always had an area of achievement that is unattainable by men—the ability to bear children. Many experts have argued that this often leads to an unconscious envy that is so intense that it is at the very root of men's feelings of inferiority. Men spend their whole lives trying to compensate for their inability to directly perpetuate the species. Some social scientists have even gone so far as to suggest that women's childbearing capacity is the root of all of men's fears.

All told, men who still promote women's purported secondary status do not have much evidence to base it on. This is not to say that women are innately superior to men. On the contrary, there are a number of arenas in which men excel. Most obvious is their physical strength. If you don't see men and women competing one-on-one in sporting events, it's because there is little doubt that women would be clobbered. Men are also ahead of the game when it comes to mechanical skills. A woman can certainly learn to understand the internal workings of an automobile, but chances are, it will take her longer to figure things out than an equally intelligent man. Again, we're not saying that women cannot learn these skills—they are just more difficult for women to master.

How then would the scale tip if we could measure which sex is innately superior? Most likely, it wouldn't tip at all. Whatever men—or women—would like to believe, the sexes are different but overall they are equal—a fact of life that chills most Samsons to the bone. To most men, equality with women feels the same as being inferior to them.

Why do men feel that if they are not superior then they must, by definition, be inferior? Why do they experience, as Karen Horney put it, "everything falling short of complete domination . . .

as subjugation"?[30] Some of it has to do with the fact that a boy never quite gets over the fact that his mother was once omnipotent. Unconsciously, he always harbors the fear that if he does not control women, he will ultimately be controlled *by* them.

The real heart of the problem, however, is that although women have a sure-fire way of proving their femininity by having babies, a man's masculinity is never confirmed once and for all. As we discussed earlier, a large part of being masculine is not being feminine—a kind of negative definition of self. This leaves men in a position in which they have to prove and redefine their manhood over and over again. Most often, the way they prove it is by believing themselves to be superior to women and acting out that belief.

Nancy Chodorow, in her wonderful book *The Reproduction of Mothering*, sums it up well: "Given that masculinity is so elusive, it becomes important for masculine identity that certain social activities are defined as masculine and superior, and that women are believed unable to do many of the things defined as socially important. It becomes important to think that women's economic and social contribution cannot equal men's."[31]

Simply put, a woman does not have to be a castrating bitch for a man to feel castrated by her: all she has to do is act like his equal.

This is why men go to such great lengths to prove that women are inferior to men and why, given the greater opportunities that are opening up for women, the game can get so downright dirty.

Where Has All This Fear Been for So Long?

At this point, you are probably wondering, "If so many men are afraid of women, how has the fear gone unnoticed for so long?" The answer is that men have built a psychological and social fortress behind which they have hidden their fear both from women and from themselves. In the following chapter, we will discuss the building materials of that fortress, detailing the defenses men have used to keep their fear from surfacing, and what happens when they find that their defenses no longer work.

Chapter 2

The Blockade Against Fear

Do you know a Samson? Almost every women we spoke to was sure that she did. But sensing a man's fear is one thing; zeroing in on the characteristics of a true Samson is more difficult than it would initially seem to be.

We will present a test in Chapter 3 in order to help you to determine if any of the men in your life fall into the Samson category, but there are a number of reasons that categorizing a man as a Samson isn't always easy. Part of the problem is that it is a matter of degree: some men are deathly afraid of everything about women, while others experience a more moderate level of fear, and still others, no fear at all. Also, while some men experience all the fears we discussed in the last chapter, others are afraid of women in some ways but not in others. A man might not have the slightest fear of being controlled by women sexually, but he may be paranoid about being emotionally rejected or abandoned. Or he may feel confident that the woman in his life will never leave him, while harboring earthshaking feelings of inferiority and inadequacy in relation to the women he works with.

To complicate things further, some men are "closet" Samsons. These are men who boast of their egalitarian attitudes and who firmly believe that they are as liberated as they think they are but who simply have not as yet found themselves in situations that trigger their fear. Philip M., whose story is discussed in detail in Chapter 7, is a case in point. At the time he married Leslie, a struggling artist, he appeared to be totally unafraid of her success. In fact, her ambition, he told us, was one of the reasons he married her. It was only after she started becoming successful that the volcano of his fear erupted. But what if his wife had never become successful, had remained a struggling artist? Chances are, he might have been able to hide the Samson that lurked within for the rest of his life.

Nor can you assume that a man who holds relatively traditional values is a Samson, although there is often a link. Believing that it's better for a mother to stay at home with preschoolers doesn't make a man a Samson, any more than espousing support for the women's movement makes a man unafraid of women.

By far the most problematic aspect in labeling a man a true Samson is the fact that his fear most often doesn't look like fear. A few men might openly reveal their fear to a woman or admit to their fear behind the doors of a therapist's office. But many men come across so confidently, so definitely superior when it comes to women, that they do not appear to be fearful at all. Who would think that a man who is vice president of a multimillion-dollar corporation secretly worries that he is inferior to the woman who is his protégé? Who would guess that a Don Juan, who exudes confidence and poise, is deathly afraid of being rejected? What would make you suspect that the man who hops from bed to bed, refusing to make a commitment to any woman, is, in his heart of hearts, afraid of his utter dependence on them?

Given all these complications, how can you separate the man who fears women from the man who does not? How do you tell the difference between a true Samson and a man who is simply having difficulty adjusting to the rapidly changing roles of men and women?

Denial is often a good first clue. The man who does not harbor an underlying fear of women but who is experiencing some difficulty in adjusting to recent sex-role changes is usually quite conscious of his discomfort. "When my wife recently received a promotion and began making more than I do, I experienced a twinge of uneasiness," one man admitted. "I guess on some level I felt that I was somehow less of a man if I made less than she; that I was somehow inferior to her. And it bothered me." At the same time, he told us that he knew that to act on his feelings would be destructive to his relationship with his wife, who he considers his best friend. "I guess you could say that I just talked myself out of my feelings of inadequacy." He then blushed and added, "Well, at least I've mostly overcome it. I still feel inadequate from time to time, you know a little less 'a man,' but I don't let that feeling run my life or my relationship with Gina."

A man like this who can openly admit that he feels "funny" or "uncomfortable" about the new role prescriptions for men and women is not a Samson but a man who is reacting to change. He can admit that he feels somewhat threatened, yet at the same time he can take control of his feelings. The true Samson does neither. Ask him if he feels afraid of women or threatened by them, and he'll deny it until he's blue in the face. "Who me? Afraid? Threatened by women?" is the typical response. "Who are you kidding?" He does not realize that in his staunch denial he all but gives himself away.

There is another reliable way of differentiating the Samson from the non-Samson. The non-Samson has no need to dominate or control the women in his life or to continually prove his superiority to them. For the Samson, subjugating and controlling women is almost a way of life. When he begins feeling that control slipping through his fingers, he feels even more frightened. And the more frightened he gets, the more controlling he becomes.

The Need to Dominate: A Surefire Sign of Fear

It's a psychiatric truism that one of the best ways for a person to control his or her fear is to control the object of that fear. This psychological defense can be seen in the bully or, in its most extreme form, in the dictatorial personalities of men like Hitler or Mussolini. It is also the great facade of the Samson and Delilah Complex, behind which men's fear of being abandoned, controlled, or proven inferior to women is hidden. This fear is masked by a compensatory need to dominate that becomes stronger as the fear increases. Ashley Montagu once wrote, "The truly superior person doesn't need to lord it over anyone; it is only the inferior person who, in order to feel that he is superior, must have someone to look down on."[1] The man who isn't afraid of women doesn't need to keep women under his thumb; it is only the man who, in order to keep his fear from surfacing, must work so hard to keep women in their "place."

The true Samson not only enjoys being the one in charge, he feels that he *must* be in charge in order to keep his fear under wraps. Alfred Adler, the great psychologist who wrote extensively about fear, said this compulsive need to control was an *unhealthy* drive for superiority. Triggered by underlying and often unconscious feelings of fear, the ultimate aim of this unhealthy striving, said Adler, is to deflect the fear by demeaning or controlling others.[2] That's why a Samson is so bent on keeping women at least one rung beneath him. Unconsciously, Samson's motto is "If I control women, they cannot control me; they can never prove themselves superior to me; they can never leave me."

Defenses Against Fear

If you want to identify a Samson, you need to home in not only on his fears but also on the mechanisms of control that he uses to hide his fears. We call these strategies *the defenses against fear*. Below, we briefly review the defenses that men use to try to control women and, hence, lessen their fear of them.

Economic Dominance

Women may have come a long way, but many men still use economic dominance as a primary means of controlling their fear. The man who uses this strategy tries to dominate the woman in his life by using his greater earning power as a way of securing greater power in the relationship. Sometimes a man like this forbids his wife to work or makes working very difficult for her. If he has corporate power, he tries to bar women from positions of power in his company. Either way, economic dominance has the effect of limiting women's power, thereby lessening men's fear. After all, what is there to fear in someone who is financially insecure? How can she abandon you when she is dependent on you for her room and board?

Extreme Possessiveness

The overly possessive Samson seeks to dominate by making the woman close to him completely dependent on him psychologically. Often he comes across as a kind of mentor—helpful and supportive—but at the same time he usually tries to make a woman feel incompetent. He is jealous of everyone and everything that takes her away from him, and he often tries to restrict her contact with other people. His ploy is to make the woman in his life feel that she cannot do anything without him, that she cannot live without him.

The effectiveness of possessiveness as a defense depends a lot on whether a man's possessiveness comes across as domineering or loving. In the case of the former, a woman usually responds to possessiveness with anger and hostility. The latter, however, often gets quite the opposite response: reveling in all that love and idolization, a woman may very well succumb to her man's possessiveness, eventually becoming as dependent on him as he is on her.

Withdrawal

The Samson who uses withdrawal tries to control his fear by keeping emotionally distant from women. He hides his tremendous fear and need by acting as if he doesn't need his woman at all. He pulls away from her, often when she needs him most, and he spends most of his time away from her—working, drinking, out with the boys. Even when he is physically present, he is not really there emotionally. If he is single, he usually has tremendous problems making a commitment to any woman. If he's married, he may very well leave a trail of brief affairs behind him. He may appear to be committed to the marriage at first, but as soon as he feels too close, his emotional need is kindled and he runs away.

The withdrawn Samson may also be overly possessive at the same time. A man like this can make a woman's life truly miserable because he does not provide her with much emotional nourishment, yet at the same time he forbids her to fulfill her needs elsewhere.

Although withdrawal works well to control a man's fear, it also leaves him a victim of his own unfulfilled need to love and be loved. Feeling his distance, the woman with a withdrawing Samson tends to keep her distance from him in response. Often she leaves, if not physically, then emotionally. His fear of being abandoned becomes a self-fulfilling prophecy.

Physical Violence, Humiliation, Contempt, and Sabotage

Physical violence, humiliation, contempt, and sabotage share one common quality: domination through hostility. The Samson who humiliates a woman or who uses physical violence is trying to assault her self-esteem in the hope that she will be unable to leave him or, in a case of fear of inferiority, to show him up. The contemptuous Samson aims at much the same thing, with the added element of trying to make the woman in his life feel not only unworthy but unloved. The sabotaging Samson camouflages his fear by taking active measures to destroy the source of his fear. He may, for example, sabotage a woman on the job by starting a nasty rumor about her or by "conveniently" forgetting to pass on an important piece of information to her. Or he may sabotage his wife's success by becoming ill during the time she is most in need of his support.

Breakdown

When a man has exhausted his available defenses and is nonetheless still in a relationship with a woman who triggers his fear, he usually falls apart, that is, he breaks down. A breakdown may also be considered a last-resort defense: who would hurt someone who is so defenseless, so helpless?

Breakdown takes one of two forms. The first is a man's complete submissiveness to the whims and demands of the woman in his life. We consider this a form of breakdown because a person who is unequivocally submissive is a person who has lost himself. For a man to be utterly submissive, that loss of self is combined with a loss of manhood. Men like these are aware, as are all men, of the pejorative terms used to describe men who submit to women, who are completely dominated by them. Nevertheless, they cannot help themselves. They would rather lose their manhood than their women—if they had the choice. What they are saying is "If I do everything that you want, you will not leave me."

The second type of breakdown is more overt and manifests itself in symptoms we most typically associate with mental duress: depression, sometimes to the point of being suicidal, extreme emotional withdrawal, psychosomatic ailments—a feeling of general mental malaise, which in extreme cases may lead to psychosis or major physical ailments. When the breakdown is being used as a defense, the hidden message is "See how sick and helpless I am? Would you dare to go against my wishes now?"

Whether it's used as a defense or not, breakdown is usually a terrifying experience. This isn't to say that it can have no redeeming qualities: sometimes a man must hit rock bottom before he can begin working his way out of his predicament.

The Hierarchy of Defense

What we found most interesting about these defenses is that in many instances there was a specific pattern in which these defenses emerged. We observed time and time again that, as one defense begins to crumble or no longer works to control women and block the fear, another defense is erected in its place. We call this pattern the *hierarchy of defense*.

At the forefront of blockade is economic dominance. Controlling women by controlling the purse strings is still men's first line of defense, largely because it is socially sanctioned and available to most men. When economic dominance goes unchallenged, a man who uses this defense never has to contend with his fear. Nor does he (unless he is the most frightened of Samsons) need to erect other defenses. His fear well buttressed economically, he needs no other walls behind which to hide.

But what happens when the economic blockade is broken—a situation that is almost always triggered either by a woman's rebellion against it or by her financial success?

A second line of defense is erected, and quite often the defense is either possessiveness or withdrawal. These defenses can be as strong as economic dominance and are particularly virulent when they are combined with it. As long as this second line of defense works, the fear is stopped dead in its tracks.

When neither the first nor second line of defense is sufficient to quiet a man's fear (or when a man does not use possessiveness or withdrawal), yet other defenses are erected, including humiliation and disparagement, violence and sabotage. These third-line defense mechanisms are the most vicious, and the man who uses them is usually grasping at straws, desperately trying to control his fear.

When none of these defenses works, then what? With his strategies exhausted, the fearful Samson eventually breaks down. He is left defenseless, forced to come face to face with his fear.

The foregoing description would seem to suggest that a man who is afraid of women will move predictably from one level of defense to another. However, this is often not the case. A man may flee, either physically or emotionally, from the source of his fear as any level of defense breaks down. A man who, for example, discovers that threats of physical violence do not stop his wife from pursuing her career, which then increases his fear of being inferior, may ask for a divorce, or he may divorce himself from his wife emotionally. He adopts an "I'm not afraid, I just don't give a damn" attitude as a protection, a mask to hide his vulnerability.

A man might also break down before exhausting all three lines of defense—because not all men can defend themselves with equal effectiveness. Nor can all men successfully keep their feelings below the surface. And of course, a man might also, consciously or unconsciously, use a breakdown as a defense in and of itself.

The lines of defense thus do not necessarily occur in a sequential, step-by-step fashion. More often than not, men's defenses overlap or occur simultaneously. When a man is extremely fearful, he may use all the defenses at once, just to be on the safe side. Nor do all men use all the defenses. Some men, for example, move straight to the third-line defenses when their economic dominance is threatened. Others use a combination of second- and third-line defenses at the same time. Still others never use economic dominance as a first line of defense at all. It might be considered unacceptable in certain social circles. A man might also need his partner's economic contribution to support the family. For the single man, controlling a woman by controlling the purse strings is not viable unless she is his mistress or unless she has been involved with him for a long time and has become accustomed to a lifestyle that she herself could not afford.

Another important exception to the rule is the man who deals with his fear by pursuing exactly the kind of woman of whom he is most afraid. A man like this is usually so out of touch with his fear that he bends over backward to prove how unafraid he is.

Often he marries a bright, ambitious woman with a lot of "potential," only to sabotage or humiliate her when her career threatens to outshine his. In some cases, he just breaks down. Because he has denied his fear so thoroughly, the woman in his life is often shocked and hurt. "He seemed so supportive," one woman told us, "and then suddenly out of nowhere he began sabotaging my career." The key word here is *seemed:* if a man like this were not afraid, he would have no use for defenses at all.

Finally, a man may never move from one line of defense to another because he learns to cope with his fear. Rather than constructing more defenses when his fear is exposed, he may be able to recognize his fear (sometimes with the aid of professional counseling) as well as its deleterious effects. As a result, he might begin letting go of his need to control women because he has taken control of himself and his fear. Once again, this can happen at any stage of the defense hierarchy. It is obviously the most positive response to fear. Unfortunately, it is also a response that many men have not yet been able to make. This is sad, because a man's need to keep women down, his need to battle them, is a war he himself has made. In the process, he also makes women feel as if men are their enemies.

The Samson and Delilah Complex: A Self-Fulfilling Prophecy

The great irony of men's fear of women is this: men's need to put up defenses against their fear by keeping women down creates a breeding ground ripe for producing exactly the kind of woman that men fear most. Most women do not want to fight with men, nor do they want to overrun them; they simply want to be treated as equals. The paradox is that men's fear and their battle to defend themselves against it often make otherwise loving, devoted women into bitter rivals and foes.

It begins the moment the first defense is put into place. If a man does not try to dominate or control the woman in his life, she will have no blockade to try to break through. Not surprisingly, as a man sets up each new defense, as each new barricade is constructed, the woman in his life becomes increasingly angry. The

angrier she gets, the more likely she is to abandon her man physically or emotionally or to treat him disparagingly. And if she sticks
around long enough for him to break down, chances are she no
longer cares. Samson has confirmed his worst fears by playing a
part in creating them.

In this way, the Samson and Delilah Complex becomes a self-
fulfilling prophecy.

Chapter 3

Is Your Man a Samson?
A Test to Help You Decide

In this chapter, you will learn how to tell if a man is a Samson. To do this, you have to evaluate the defenses he may be using to hide his fear: economic dominance, possessiveness, withdrawal, humiliation, sabotage, or physical violence. The Samson Test has been designed to measure how much he uses each of these defenses. After answering each of the questions, we'll show you how to interpret the results. Remember, there are no right or wrong answers. Simply answer the questions based on your own personal experience and on how you yourself feel. The more honest you are about your situation, the more accurate your results will be.

The test has been written from the point of view of a woman observing a man with whom she has a close relationship. If you have a different relationship with the potential Samson you have in mind, change the wording of the questions accordingly. Think about each question carefully. The test includes as many common experiences as possible, but since everyone's circumstances are different, you may have to interpret the question to fit your specific situation.

Instructions are provided throughout the test. Be sure to follow them carefully.

THE SAMSON TEST

Circle the number below each statement that most accurately describes the man you are thinking about. Add up the numbers you have circled and record your score on the subtotal line at the end of each part.

Never or Rarely   Occasionally   Often   Very Often

PART I: ECONOMIC DOMINANCE

He discourages your working or going to work.

    0   1   2   3

When you have a disagreement that involves money, he uses the argument that he earns more than you do in order to get his way.

    0   1   2   3

He buys whatever he wants, but says the things you want will have to wait.

    0   1   2   3

He would feel threatened if you earned more money than he.

    0   1   2   3

ECONOMIC DOMINANCE SUBTOTAL_____

Part II: Possesssiveness

He becomes hostile, withdrawn, or whiny when you're not available to him when he wants you to be.

    0   1   2   3

He discourages you from having a close relationship with anyone outside your immediate family.

    0   1   2   3

When you speak to someone on the phone, he wants to know who you are talking to.

    0   1   2   3

He discourages relationships or activities that do not include him.

    0   1   2   3

POSSESSIVENESS SUBTOTAL _____

PART III: WITHDRAWAL

He pulls away from you emotionally or is more critical of you after you have had a positive, intimate exchange.

    0   1   2   3

He spends more of his free time drinking, watching TV, out with the "boys," or working than he spends with you.

    0   1   2   3

You get the feeling that he is behind a wall that you are not even allowed to look over.

    0   1   2   3

When you complain that he is distant or doesn't talk to you, he says that he doesn't understand what you are talking about or that you are nagging him; or else he becomes more distant.

    0   1   2   3

WITHDRAWAL SUBTOTAL _____

Part IV: Physical Violence

When he becomes angry, you feel frightened that he might harm you physically.

      0   1   2   3

He grabs, pushes, or confines you physically, or he throws things at you.

      0   1   2   3

He strikes you physically.

      0   1   2   3

He has hurt you during lovemaking or has forced you to make love when you did not want to.

      0   1   2   3

PHYSICAL VIOLENCE SUBTOTAL _____

Part V: Humiliation

When you talk about something you feel proud of, he shows no interest and makes you feel that what you've done is not important.

      0   1   2   3

He belittles your intelligence or talks to you in a condescending way.

      0   1   2   3

He says things about you in front of other people that embarrass you.

      0   1   2   3

He finds a lot of things to criticize you about.

     0   1   2   3

HUMILIATION SUBTOTAL

PART VI: SABOTAGE

He becomes dependent or needy when you are under a lot of pressure at work or school.

     0   1   2   3

The better you feel about yourself or about your accomplishments at school or on the job, the more likely he is to put you down in front of your friends or co-workers.

     0   1   2   3

He stands in the way of your getting ahead on the job or pursuing your education by wearing you down with his hostility or demands on your time.

     0   1   2   3

He refuses to share in the childrearing or household responsibilities.

     0   1   2   3

SABOTAGE SUBTOTAL＿＿＿＿＿

PART VII: OVERT BREAKDOWN

He has fits of rage for little or no apparent reason.

     0   1   2   3

He seems depressed, has no interest in sex, is impotent, or complains about being physically ill.

    0   1   2   3

He thinks that the people you associate with are against him.

    0   1   2   3

He uses alcohol or other drugs excessively.

    0   1   2   3

OVERT BREAKDOWN SUBTOTAL _____

PART VIII: COVERT BREAKDOWN: SUBMISSIVENESS

He submits to your desires in almost every way.

    0   1   2   3

As you become more assertive, he lets you order him about even more.

    0   1   2   3

When you get angry, he goes along with you just to keep the peace.

    0   1   2   3

He agrees with your opinions even when you know he really doesn't mean what he says.

    0   1   2   3

SUBMISSIVENESS SUBTOTAL _____

Now that you have completed the test, read on and learn how to interpret your scores.

Interpreting Your Samson Test Score

The key to interpreting your score is to determine where the man is in the hierarchy of defenses that we discussed in Chapter 2. You need to decipher the defenses he uses to hide his fear.

The Samson Test Results

The Defense		The Score
Part I:	Economic Dominance	_____
Part II:	Possessiveness	_____
Part III:	Withdrawal	_____
Part IV:	Physical Violence	_____
Part V:	Humiliation	_____
Part VI:	Sabotage	_____
Part VII:	Overt Breakdown	_____
Part VIII:	Covert Breakdown: Submissiveness	_____

In order to determine if your man is a Samson and what kind of Samson he is, you need to pinpoint which defense or set of defenses against fear he is utilizing, as well as the strength of those defenses. There are between 0 and 12 points that a man can score in each category.

A score of 0 to 4 in any category indicates that he may have some Samson-like traits, but chances are the man in your life is not a Samson. Perhaps, from time to time, he experiences some insecurity about how you feel about him or about his own self-worth, or he may be having some difficulty adjusting to the changing role of women. Generally speaking, however, his fear of women is probably very small.

A score of 5 to 8 in one or more categories indicates that he has a moderately strong fear of women and is trying to control or dominate you with that defense or set of defenses.

A score above 8 in any category suggests that the man in your life has a strong fear of women and a strong need to control them.

Since being a Samson is not simply an either/or evaluation but a matter of type and degree, it is also important to understand what the defenses mean when used alone and in combination with one another.

If His Score Is Above 4 for Economic Dominance and Less Than 4 for All Other Sections of the Test:

A man like this uses economic dominance as his primary line of defense. He is able to control his fear by keeping a tight grip on the purse strings. He believes that you will never leave him or show him to be inferior as long as you do not challenge his economic superiority. Most often, this means that he earns more money than you do and uses his superior earning power as a springboard to greater power in the relationship generally.

Do not deceive yourself into thinking that he is not a full-fledged Samson because he scored high on only one defense. He needs only one defense because economic dominance is strong enough to control his fear. Should you at some point challenge his economic dominance, however, you can expect some of the second- or third-line defenses to come into play.

Economic Dominance and Possessiveness or Withdrawal

A man who combines economic dominance with one of the second-line defenses—possessiveness or withdrawal—is more fearful than the man who uses economic dominance alone. Either he feels that his economically dominant position is threatened, or he is so afraid of women that he needs more than one defense to assuage his fear. If he is possessive and economically dominant, he is so fearful that he needs to control both the purse strings *and* your personal life. If he is economically dominant and withdrawn, he may be trying to buy off his inability to be emotionally intimate with material things.

Economic Dominance and Physical Violence, Humiliation, and Sabotage

A man like this is truly a full-fledged Samson. Not only does he need to control you economically, he must also keep you in your place by putting you down or otherwise standing in the way of your becoming more self-sufficient as a person. In extreme cases, he may become violent and harm you physically. (Sometimes he may be possessive or withdrawn as well.) He is a man whose fear is out of control.

Possessiveness or Withdrawal Only

A man who is not economically dominant may rely on possessiveness as a first line of defense. However, if you decide that you will no longer tolerate his possessiveness, he may become humiliating, sabotaging, or even violent.

Similarly, withdrawal is used as a defense by itself when economic dominance is not viable. Most often, a man who falls into this pattern is single. He avoids his fear of being dependent on or abandoned by women by pulling away from them emotionally. He controls women by always being the one in the driver's seat emotionally. If a woman challenges his inability to give emotionally, he usually does not adopt another defense but ends the relationship instead.

Possessiveness or Withdrawal and Physical Violence, Humiliation, and Sabotage

A man like this is a man who is desperately fearful of women. Usually the only reason that he does not try to control a woman economically is because he is not in a position to do so, or she does not allow him to do so.

Humiliation and/or Physical Violence or Sabotage Only

He is desperate to control his fear. Almost always, this pattern of defense is found among men who have been stripped of all other defenses. He tries to dominate by using one or more of these defenses as a last resort. His fear has completely run away with him. If a woman refuses to tolerate any of these control mechanisms, chances are that he will completely break down.

Overt Breakdown

A man breaks down, that is, becomes dysfunctional, for a variety of reasons; fear of women is only one of them. The best clue to determining if a man's breakdown is related to fear of women is whether he has unsuccessfully used the defenses mentioned above in the past. It is when he is unable to call forth any other defenses to control his fear that the breakdown often occurs.

As we noted earlier, breakdown can occur in combination with other defenses. This usually suggests that a man's fear is so intense that the standard defenses are unable to contain it. A man like this needs therapeutic treatment in order to recover.

This confrontation with fear may, on the other hand, be a primary motivating factor in overcoming it and in avoiding a complete psychological breakdown. It depends on how dysfunctional a Samson becomes.

Covert Breakdown: Submissiveness

A man who becomes utterly submissive after one or all of the other defenses have failed to quell his fear is a man who is experiencing a covert form of breakdown. He is so afraid of losing the woman in his life that he will do anything she wants in his attempt to keep her. If his submissiveness is successful; that is, if a woman stays with him once he becomes submissive, a more overt breakdown may be avoided. Should the woman reject his submissiveness, however, there is a real possibility that he will suffer a more overt breakdown.

The man whose submissiveness is a manifestation of a covert breakdown should not be confused with a man who has always been submissive to women. Unlike the man who becomes submissive only after his other defenses have failed, a man who has always been submissive uses submissiveness as a first line of defense against fear.

In the chapters that follow, we will discuss men's defenses and their need to control women in detail. In Part II, we will tell you what you can do to help a Samson overcome his fear.

Chapter 4

The First Line of Defense: Economic Dominance

Caroline, a twenty-nine-year-old wife and mother of two, admits that she has, on more than one occasion, felt dissatisfied with her eight-year marriage to her husband, Donald. He's not a bad man, she says, but there is something lacking—a certain spark, a certain feeling of companionate intimacy. But ask Caroline if she has ever considered leaving Donald, and she answers with her eyes, which travel from the dirty dishes in the sink, to her four-year-old whose energy never seems to abate, to her infant who cries restlessly in her arms, to the stack of bills on the kitchen table that she pays with her husband's salary each month. Caroline never went to college, but she is no ignoramus when it comes to understanding her own predicament. "One does not bite the hand that feeds, you know," she says.

We know. And on some level, so do most men. Throughout history, keeping women socially and economically manacled has been the means by which men have controlled women and calmed their own fears. Keeping women economically disabled is the first line of defense for many Samsons, even in today's so-called emancipated society.

For some men, economic superiority is a defense against the fear of inferiority. As author Marilyn French puts it, a sense of superiority and control over women is crucial to a man's self-esteem. It forces men to demonstrate their superiority by "imposing on women deprivations which imprison them in a condition seen as inferior by the male."[1] Men impose their will, they keep women in a subservient position, by means of economic control.

Other men use economic control to ameliorate their fear of being sexually controlled. For men like these, supporting a woman economically is a direct exchange: if she gives him what he needs sexually, he will give her what she wants economically.

Still other Samsons use economic dominance as a defense against the fear of being abandoned or rejected. Deep down, many men are afraid that, money aside, women can get along just fine without them. That's why they are often so insistent on holding the purse strings and why they feel so threatened by economically self-sufficient women. Without the security blanket of his economic reins, says psychiatrist Wolfgang Lederer in *The Dread of Women*, a man is likely to feel that he is "left weaponless," that "if she does not at least need him for something, he has no hold over her at all."[2]

Unconsciously, the Samson who needs to keep a woman in an economically inferior position knows that a dependent woman does not just get up and walk out. Nor does a dependent woman threaten a man's need to prove his superiority. After all, how could anyone be threatened by someone who can't even pay her own way? Knowing that he cannot control his sexual and emotional vulnerability to women or his fear of inferiority to them, his only way of controlling her is to make a woman dependent on him for her everyday survival.

Think of how different the Samson and Delilah story would have been had Delilah depended on Samson for her economic well-being. Indeed, the whole Samson-Delilah saga would have had to be rewritten if Delilah, rather than being an independently wealthy priestess, had been a woman whose only means of financial support was Samson.

Imagine, for a moment, that Delilah is an average homemaker with two young children. Perhaps she married right out of high school and never developed any skills applicable to the job market. Or maybe she worked as a secretary for a while, or as a teacher, but during the years she stayed home to raise her young children, her job skills became rusty. Either way, she needs Samson for her economic security. Deep down she knows that her ability to support herself is shaky. She also knows that her ability to support herself in the manner to which she's become accustomed, given Samson's salary, is probably an impossible dream.

In a nutshell, Delilah-as-average-woman would have needed a Samson to take care of her and her children. She would never, even if she had dreamed of it, have betrayed or abandoned him, because the reality is that she could not have *afforded* to.

Many men still count on that reality, guarding their economically superior position with great zeal. Women may have come a long way, but the view that many men hold of working women hasn't changed as much over the years as you might think. In a nationwide study that led to their book *American Couples,* Drs. Pepper Schwartz and Philip Blumstein found that more men cherished the idea of the breadwinner/homemaker division of labor than believed that both partners in the relationship should work. Even men whose wives did work often accepted their wives' breadwinner status with less than wholehearted enthusiasm.[3] Other studies point in the same direction: men may talk a good line about equality for women, but when it comes down to it, many men are still looking for the traditional, subservient wife.[4]

Nor has the way that men use the social structure to keep women economically disadvantaged undergone much alteration. Women may be entering the labor force in increasing numbers, but over the past ten years, women earn less, relative to men, than they did ten years ago! In recent years, alimony has increasingly been viewed with disfavor for all "able-bodied women," even for women who have been out of the labor force for many years to raise their children. While there has been some talk about Social Security and financial remuneration for homemakers, legislators just can't seem to drum up any real support for the idea. Then, of course, there is the ever-increasing need for reasonably priced child care—a need that both the government and private industry largely continue to ignore.

Even men who think of themselves as relatively liberated often exist in a kind of intellectual-emotional schism. They fluctuate between rationally understanding that women have the right to economic parity and emotionally feeling that that right is a threat to them. "It's as if my mind says one thing and my gut says another" is the way one man explained it. "Equality is the American way, right? So of course I think that women should have the right to work and the right to equal pay for equal work. But when my wife told me that she was going to get a job, I felt . . . threatened. The worst part about it was that I couldn't reconcile my feelings with the way that I thought I should be feeling about it."

At least this man has an inkling of his fear, which means that he has taken the first step to overcome it. But most Samsons are so out of touch with their fear that they need to build defense upon defense in order to hide it.

It's important to emphasize that not all men who believe that the man should be the predominant breadwinner are Samsons. There are some men who truly believe that the homemaker's role is an invaluable one and who prefer having their wives at home when the children are young. Still others think that a dual-career family suffers from having no one to be the primary emotional guardian of the family. They view part-time work as a better option for the homemaker who wants to expand her horizons than a full-time job or a full-fledged career.

How, then, can you distinguish this pseudo-Samson from the more tried and true variety?

Dominance vs. Equality

The main ingredient found in the true Samson that differentiates him from his traditional yet non-Samson counterpart is that the real Samson uses his superior economic standing as a springboard for power in the relationship. This can occur whether a woman is employed or not, as long as he earns more than she does, which is still usually the case even if she holds the same job as he does. The issue is not whether she has an income but whether her spouse uses his greater earning power as a claim to greater power in the relationship as a whole.

The experience of one nonworking woman suggests that her man is *not* a Samson. "My husband makes a good salary, and he really is glad that I don't want to work outside the home. We have two school-aged children, and I'm very involved with their school activities and have a lot of time to spend with them when they come home. My husband considers my job as important as his. In fact, sometimes he says that he thinks that what a mother and wife does is a lot more worthwhile than being a breadwinner. And even though I don't produce an income, we share equally in all the decisions. We're partners, and when we disagree about something, we haggle it out. He never says, 'I make the money, so I call the shots.' "

Now listen to a working woman whose response suggests an entirely different attitude. "My husband doesn't mind the fact that I work, at least so he says. The thing is that he makes a lot more than I do—he's a lawyer and I'm a dental hygienist—and he's always using the fact of his larger income to get his way. For instance, he recently went out and bought an expensive new car without discussing it with me. I thought that wasn't fair, and told him so. And you know what he said? 'When you make the kind of money that I do, you can have equal say in how it's spent.' And from his point of view, that's the end of that.

"The other thing that he does," she continued, "is make me feel as if my work is not making a contribution to the household. We have a four-year-old, and it's true that day care is very expensive, but somehow he sees that expense as coming out of *my* salary. So whenever I ask him to help me out because I'm tired, he'll say that it's not his responsibility, that I could just as well stay at home with what I clear after expenses. That makes me feel very angry and very insignificant."

As resentful as she feels, she is not entirely surprised. "The truth is, he's held money over my head from the start," she told us. "When we got married, we decided that I would move into the house he had been living in for a few years. That was fine with me—it's a great house. But you know, he never let me forget that it was *his*. He wouldn't let me bring any of my own furniture, because *his* furniture was better. He didn't let me redecorate, because *his* taste was better. He's always been like that, but I guess until recently I didn't want to see it."

The essential difference between the first woman's experience and the second is that in the first there is a sense of fifty-fifty, what psychologists sometimes refer to as *reciprocal relations*. The first woman does not earn a cent, yet her husband not only respects her, he views her as an equally competent partner. He does not hold his earning power over her head, nor does he treat her as a second-class member of their relationship. (However, there is no way to tell what would happen if this woman did begin earning her own income, no way to know for sure if there is a closet Samson lurking beneath this egalitarian exterior.)

The second woman, on the other hand, tells a very different tale. Her husband may not forbid her to work, as other Samsons do, but there's no doubt that her Samson uses his superior economic power as a way to exert greater power within the total relationship. A man like this considers himself the primary decision maker in the family, particularly when it comes to money. Moreover, he will often use his role as the primary breadwinner as a way to get out of housework and other day-to-day responsibilities if the family cannot afford to hire outside help. It doesn't matter that his wife works as many hours as he: he makes more money, and sees his time, both on and off the job, as more valuable than hers. Homemaking is her job, and it is one that is clearly beneath him.

If his wife announces her intentions to work or to accept a more time-consuming job at better pay, a Samson like this usually starts out by defining, in no uncertain terms, what he will or, more aptly, what he will not do, should she go to work. He will not be one of those "henpecked" men who shares equally in "women's work." He will continue to expect a clean house, well-scrubbed children, and a home-cooked meal. He will not take on more child-care responsibilities or be available to take off from work should their child become ill. Basically, what he is saying is, "If you are foolish enough to want to take on two full-time jobs, go to it."

A Samson's need to domineer makes him unable to have a fifty-fifty relationship or to recognize that his wife's contribution to the family is as important as his is. As psychoanalyst Karen Horney put it, his fear puts him in a place where "he either has to lead or he feels entirely lost, dependent, helpless."[5] The fact that this autocratic control is a cover-up for weakness and fear does little to assuage the anger and resentment of the woman toward whom it is directed. These feelings of anger and resentment are decidedly missing in relationships where money is not used as a source of control.

Rationalization

The second ingredient that separates the man who is using economic dominance as a defense from the man who is not is his ability to listen to reason. When a non-Samson hears an argument, he considers it in rational terms. But when the fearful man hears the voice of reason, he comes up with a long list of "reasons" of his own that ignore the facts in order to confirm his view of reality.

The list of rationalizations men use to try to maintain their economically dominant positions is endless, but in our research we found three to be most common.

Women Can't Take the Heat

One such rationalization is that women are simply not strong enough to bear the pressures of a "man's" world. On the one hand, there are those Samsons who insist that women are weak and intellectually inferior, who demean women in order to make themselves feel superior. Then there are Samsons who laud the qualities of the feminine sex, claiming that to place such fragile, delicate creatures in the dog-eat-dog world of work would only destroy their femininity. Either way, these men always have a way of getting around the facts. Show them conclusive data that women have more stamina than men and are equally intelligent, and they dismiss it as some off-the-wall research. Put them in an office where the majority of women are performing effectively, and they'll find the one or two who are incompetent. Show them that housewives are, on the whole, more depressed than working mothers, and they are likely to say that that is because working mothers are too neurotic to even realize how depressed they really are. Weak, foolish, and invalid arguments, but they are the profound beliefs of many fearful Samsons.

A Mother's Place Is with Her Children—Always

A second rationalization that men use to maintain their economically superior position is that every child needs a full-time mother. We are not talking about men who feel that young children are better off with a full-time caretaker at home (a lot of mothers think so, too) but about men who insist that any time spent away from Mom will forever damage a child's mental health. The fact that all the research shows this to be a nonsensical idea makes no difference to him.

Nichole Morton's experience is a case in point. When she married Paul, both agreed that she would quit her job when she had their first child. This she did. But when some physical problems ruled out the possibility of a second child, and Nichole's son was old enough to enter nursery school, Nichole had the desire to go back to work. So she approached Paul about getting a job.

"Over my dead body" was his response. "We had an agreement, and I expect you to live by it."

"We agreed that I should stay home when our children were very young," Nichole responded, "but Robbie's almost four now, and there are a lot of good pre-K programs around here."

"Haven't you followed the news lately?" he countered with a sneer, implying that Nichole was a half-wit. "Look at all those kids who are being sexually abused. What kind of mother would do that to her child?"

"Well, I could check very carefully into the programs."

"I said no, and that's final."

So ended round one.

Nichole's second request came a month before the Christmas holiday. "There are some openings at Penney's for people to work over the holiday, and my mother said she'd watch Robbie," said Nichole, broaching the subject.

"Forget it. Robbie needs you *here.*"

"But *why?* It's only for a few weeks, and we could really use the money. The washing machine is about to go, and our savings account is almost nonexistent."

"So we'll have to do without. It's much more important that our son have a mom at home to give him a sense of security."

"My mom worked and raised me, and I turned out all right," Nichole had wanted to scream, but instead she retreated into silence.

Then came what appeared to be Nichole's golden opportunity. Her neighbor, a close friend, gave birth to a little boy, but unlike Nichole and Paul, who could make ends meet without Nichole's having to work, Barbara desperately needed a job. Not wanting to leave her baby with a stranger, Barbara asked Nichole if she would watch Kevin at her house. Nichole was elated. After all, what could be more perfect than to work in her own home? How could Paul possibly object?

Paul found a reason. "If you spend time watching someone else's kid, you won't have enough time for your own."

"But, Paul, it would be the same way if we had another baby. Besides, Robbie doesn't need my undivided attention all the time."

"We didn't bring a child into the world so he could be raised by a part-time mother," Paul sneered as he walked away. "The subject is closed."

Women Don't Really Want to Work, Anyway

A third and increasingly common rationalization used by many Samsons is that it is not they who are holding women back from becoming economically equal, but women themselves. Now it is true that there are many women who don't want to work, and when this is the case, the man who says "I'm not stopping her; she just isn't interested" is simply stating a fact. But when one is dealing with the rationalizing Samson, the situation is different. His partner may tell him that she is miserable at home all the time, that she would like to find work. But a Samson doesn't hear her. Or, more aptly stated, he hears the words, but he *chooses* not to believe them.

What a man like this is really doing is hiding his fear by transferring it to someone else. Rather than say "I am afraid," he rationalizes his fear by claiming that she really isn't interested in economic self-sufficiency, that deep down she wants to leave the economic driving up to him.

This kind of rationalization is particularly prevalent among men who earn high incomes, and it is often combined with a kind of financial bribery.

We met a group of men like this at a focus group we ran on the Upper West Side of New York City. The men were all in their middle thirties and had prestigious, well-paying positions. Dan was a securities analyst; Norman, a dermatologist; Lloyd and Sal were both lawyers. These men spoke with a certain feeling of pride about how well they took care of their wives. All had fabulously comfortable housing. Their children went to private schools and expensive camps in the summer, while their wives luxuriated on Fire Island, an expensive summer resort. They were convinced that they had given their wives everything that they could possibly want.

"I can't imagine why Lori would want to work," Dan said. "She has the life of a princess."

The others chuckled. They knew full well that their wives had become accustomed to a cushy way of life that they would be loath to give up. "Why would my wife possibly want to work?" Lloyd questioned. "I mean, what could she do—get a job working for someone else for fifteen thousand a year? That's a pittance compared to what I make, and it would only make her feel inferior."

Had their wives ever expressed an interest in working? we wondered. "Oh, sure," Sal blurted, "Claire talks about it a lot. She says someday she'd like to open up a dress boutique. But I don't really believe it. She'd have to start at the bottom, and I don't think she's motivated enough."

Norman and Dan nodded. "Cindy often says that she doesn't know who she is, that she has a need to get out and 'find' herself," Norman offered, "but frankly I haven't the vaguest idea of what she's talking about. She's married to a famous doctor and is the mother of three active children. She gets to meet a lot of important people all the time. I think that all this women's lib stuff has gotten into her head. But she's a down-to-earth girl, and it will pass. I mean, no one is content all the time."

Only Lloyd seemed to have a glimmer of understanding that his wife might not be the happy housewife he so much wanted to believe she was. "Sometimes Julia complains about our marriage. She says that we're not as close as she'd like us to be because I work so hard. But hell, she knew that I was ambitious when I met her, so I don't know what she's complaining about."

What does he do when his wife expresses her discontent? Lloyd smirked, with a look of vague recognition about the real truth of his dilemma crossing his face. "I take her on a vacation or buy her a fancy negligee or a new diamond bracelet. That seems to calm her down, at least for a while."

All these men's responses demonstrate the way a Samson uses rationalization to maintain his economic supremacy. You can tell him over and over again that his reactions do not make sense, but he will refute you every time and put a lot of energy into proving you entirely wrong. Wasn't so-and-so's child molested in pre-K? Don't you know that kids become all screwed up when their mothers work? What interest could a financially comfortable woman have in working for someone else? Instead of admitting that irrational elements pervade his attitude, which, consequently, would force him to confront his fear, a Samson rationalizes his fears away and thereby escapes them.

Unlike the man cited earlier who could acknowledge some real uneasiness about his wife's working, a Samson continues to run and continues to hide. Suggest that he might be afraid, and he adamantly denies it or laughs it off: "What? Me afraid?"

The Seeds for Delilah Are Planted

Yet he is afraid. As Karen Horney pointed out, the more vigorously a man defends a set of irrational attitudes, the stronger is his fear.[6] Even more disturbing, his rationalizations, his need to hide his fear behind his economic superiority, often blind him to the increasing unhappiness of the woman who shares his life. "When I first brought up the idea of going to work full time, my husband had a fit," one woman told us. "He refused to discuss it. I begged him, I pleaded with him, I told him I was going out of my mind at home, but it didn't make any difference. It became clear to me after a while that he didn't give a damn about my feelings or about me."

That may be how it looks, but it usually isn't so. What is true is that his fear runs so deep that it overrides everything—even his wife's happiness.

The cruel paradox—cruel to both parties—is that in order for a Samson to keep his wife in an economically inferior position, he must continue to have both a wife and an income that allow him to do so. A woman may not know how to stand up to a man because she is economically dependent on him, and so she allows herself to be economically dominated. Yet although a Samson might successfully squelch his fear by keeping the woman in his life dependent and vulnerable, he often leaves her very unhappy. This unhappiness may eventually cause her to leave him, if not physically, then emotionally. Or she may begin demeaning him, relating to him in a hostile way. This resentment can turn a once-loving woman into a Delilah.

The Emergence of a Closet Samson

For as long as she could remember, Diane Barnes's conception of the ideal husband was a man who believed that a wife's place was right alongside her husband as an equal. She wanted the kind of relationship in which she and her husband would share equitably in both the decisions and responsibilities of the family.

When she met Ted at the beginning of her junior year of college, she was convinced she had found her dream man. They talked for hours, and found each other fascinating and stimulating. Their physical desire for one another was nothing short of passionate. Most important, Ted did not seem to have the need or desire to always be the one in the driver's seat of their relationship, as had other men Diane had dated. On the contrary, Ted viewed the traditional economic prescriptions for masculinity as a kind of harness: having sole financial responsibility for the well-being of a family was a noose he had no interest in wearing.

Deeply in love, they decided to marry the next year. Of course, there was the problem of finances—both were still students. They agreed that Ted would quit school and support them while Diane finished her bachelor's degree, and then Diane would work while Ted went back to school.

Upon graduation, Diane found a job as a public relations assistant, and Ted returned to school. After completing his degree, Ted expressed a desire to get his M.B.A., and Diane was more than happy to support his education. She loved her job and had been recently promoted to full account executive. Her salary was nothing earth-shattering, but it certainly was more than sufficient to support the two of them. Besides, Diane figured that a happy husband is a good husband, and if an advanced degree was what Ted wanted, she would be right by his side supporting him.

His M.B.A. under his belt, Ted landed an excellent entry-level position in a large corporation. The couple had worked hard, and it was paying off. Both continued to receive periodic raises and to advance professionally. They used the money they saved to put a down payment on a house, bought furniture, and took frequent vacations. They were financially comfortable, they liked their work, and they were still in love with one another.

A few years passed, and they had a baby. Ted and Diane were ecstatic. Both had agreed on the importance of a strong mother-child bond, and Diane took full advantage of the four months' maternity leave offered by her company. She enjoyed the novelty of motherhood. But when her maternity leave was almost exhausted and Diane began looking for a housekeeper, Ted expressed opposition to her going back to work. "You seem so content," he told her, "and Zachary is still so small. Why don't you quit?"

"But I've spent so long building my position in the company," Diane protested.

"A talented person is always in demand," Ted countered.

After further discussion, Diane told her employer that she would not be returning to work. She didn't really mind; Zachary was precious, and she was enthralled with him—an adoration Ted did not miss.

"Sometimes I think that you love Zachary more than you love me," Ted would say jealously.

"Don't be ridiculous," Diane would answer flippantly, since she did not understand the depths of jealousy that a man can feel toward the child who takes away the attention of the woman in his life.[7]

In the next year, Diane went from executive to full-fledged mom and homemaker. Never having been one for domestic endeavors, she was surprised at how much she enjoyed it. But as Zachary approached his first birthday, the itch to work returned. Once again, she began looking for suitable child care. Once again, Ted opposed her, this time more vehemently.

"You should at least wait until he's in school," Ted argued.

"But, Ted, I'm unhappy just staying at home. I really do need to work."

"Look, you are the mother, and as far as I'm concerned, it's your job to stay home. As it is, you already don't have enough time for me. If you wanted to have a career, then you shouldn't have had a child."

"I couldn't believe what I was hearing," Diane said. "I thought children were supposed to make a marriage closer. Instead, having a baby was tearing us apart. It was as if he were saying that I could be a mother or a breadwinner but not both. I can't imagine what turned this supposedly liberated man into a chauvinist."

Ted was not a chauvinist, but a Samson who was brought out of the closet by the birth of his child. Nor is he unusual. A number of women that we interviewed told us that their partner's egalitarian attitudes flew out the window once they had children. It has long been recognized that the primary reason men are so possessive of their superior status in the working world is because on an unconscious level they feel inferior regarding women's ability to bear and nurture children. Women are able to be executives, but men will never be able to have babies. This biological fact of life has led men to develop an area of achievement to call their own: namely, success in the working world. More "liberated" men may share their domain with their partners until the children come. But with the birth of a child, the unconscious thought of the male is, "She can do something that I cannot. Therefore, I must do something she cannot in order to keep a sense of balance. She can assert her femininity by having a child. I, too, must have an exclusive domain in which to assert my masculinity."

Added to this, the special mother-child bond dredges up men's early fear of being rejected. According to psychoanalyst Karen Horney, men's fear of women largely stems from their early dependence on and fear of rejection by their mother.[8] The birth of a child and a mother's involvement with her baby restimulates this fear. Like Ted, a man often feels excluded from the closeness a mother shares with her child; unconsciously, he feels rejected. He may also wonder, "Now that I have given her a child, and she does not need me to take care of her economically, what does she need me for?"

This theory explains why an egalitarian man may emerge as a Samson once he and his mate start a family. The sad thing is that a man's fear and his attempt to control his wife often create a self-fulfilling prophecy. Feeling suffocated, and aware that the man in her life does not care about her needs, she begins to think about leaving him. (If she had been given the freedom to make her own choice about working, she would have remained perfectly content in the relationship.)

That is precisely what happened to Diane. "Every time I brought up the issue of working, Ted made my life miserable. Things got so bad that he said the marriage would be over if I went back to work." Not wanting to raise a young child herself, Diane submitted to Ted's control and stayed at home. Turning much of her anger inward, she became depressed. Still, a considerable residue of resentment that she harbored toward her husband continued to fester. "Here was this man I had once loved dearly," Diane said. "At that point, the only feeling I had toward him was contempt. I dealt with all of this by pulling away from him. Physically, I was still there. But emotionally, I was divorced."

Diane's story epitomizes what happens when a woman allows herself to be dominated by a Samson against her wishes. Some women, unable to tolerate a man's control, end the marriage. Others, like Diane, leave the marriage without ever setting foot out the door. From the Samson's vantage point, exercising his control has alleviated his fear. What he does not realize is that what he has really done is given himself even more cause to be afraid.

Which leaves one important point unresolved. Like Diane, some women allow men to maintain their economic dominance, albeit resentfully, thereby keeping a man's fear from emerging. But what would have happened if Diane had rebelled and gone to work against Ted's wishes or if, by chance, she had started earning more than her husband? How does a Samson react when his economic dominance begins to falter and crumble?

Looking for the Next Dependent

Some men, usually those who are the most afraid, confirm women's worst fears and flee, only to marry a more dependent woman. "I think that explains a lot about why older men are often attracted to younger women," Angela Fox told us. "Sure, it has something to do with men's egos, but I also think a lot of it has to do with the fact that older women tend to be less dependent, less willing to follow orders. They are more autonomous. A young woman is more likely to be the kind of woman that a Samson wants because her dependency allows him to keep his fear under wraps."

Jim Tiers was such a man. At forty-eight, he was twice divorced; he had left each wife at the point where she became "too independent." Jim agreed to be interviewed for this book, but he totally disagreed with its premise. He told us, "It's not a matter of fear at all. I just love taking care of Tina, financially, emotionally, in every way, and she loves being taken care of. It's a perfect relationship." To prove his point, he invited us over for brunch to meet this "little darling." Tina, it turned out, was nineteen and had married Jim right after she had graduated high school. But she sounded more as if she were in grade school—there was an unnerving childishness about her high-pitched squeal and her long, banana-curled ponytail. She hung on to Jim's every word like the gospel. And whenever she was asked a question directly, her response was inevitably, "I'm not sure—what do you think, dear?" It became stunningly clear that Jim had married not an equal but a dependent. It was also clear that when it came to worries about being abandoned or about being shown to be inferior, Jim didn't have any. Rather than deal with his fear, he simply got rid of its source.

The Less-Fearful Samson

Of course, all men do not run away in the face of their fear. Many men can and do adjust. That's because the degree of fear varies from man to man. When the fear is not overpowering, a man, over time, may very well adapt. He may begin to understand that an economically dominant position is a lot less important than his wife's happiness when it comes to dealing with his fears.

Diane's husband Ted was one such man. After three years, during which her depression became increasingly worse, Diane felt that she had no alternative but to return to work, and she did so. She knew her marriage was on the line, but so was her sanity.

Diane's decision ignited a powder keg of hostility. Over dinner, Ted either stewed silently or attacked her for one reason or another. When Zachary became ill with pneumonia for two weeks, Ted refused to take off any time from work, nearly costing Diane her job. They argued constantly. The battle continued for six months.

Then, during one of his now-common tirades, Ted accused Diane of ruining their marriage. To which Diane responded, "What marriage? I don't feel as if we've had any kind of relationship for years."

"So why don't you divorce me?" Ted shot back.

"Don't think the idea hasn't crossed my mind."

"I never realized you were that unhappy," Ted said as he sat hunched on the couch in a state of shock at Diane's statement.

"I've been trying to tell you that, but you haven't listened. I just don't want to stay home all day, and I greatly resented your wanting me to when it made me so unhappy. And I continue to resent the way you have treated me since I did what I had to do for my own well-being. I was wrong to have given in to you in the first place," Diane admitted, "but you should know this: I am going to continue working. I'm sorry that you don't like the idea, but that isn't going to change my mind."

Her assertiveness that night marked the beginning of a change. Ted did not stop wanting Diane to stay at home, but he did stop making her miserable because of her decision. On some level, too, he must have recognized that his fear—whether it was wrought out of underlying feelings of inferiority or out of the fear of abandonment—was irrational. At the very least, he knew that it was not as compelling as the now-all-too-real fear of losing Diane. Most important, Diane had clearly let Ted know that she was no longer going to allow him to control her. Given her stance, Ted had one of two options: he could destroy his marriage, or he could find some way to adjust to the situation.

He adjusted, although it took some time. A year later, Diane says that Ted still gets angry sometimes about her working. Occasionally, when she works late, she comes home to find dirty pots, pans, and dinner dishes strewn about. But for the most part, their marriage is once again on solid ground. "I am a lot happier, and I can therefore make Ted a lot happier. He gets the cause-and-effect relationship between the two."

Still, when Diane thinks back to the man she married and to the man that emerged after Zachary's birth, she has difficulty fathoming the change. "There's no doubt that Ted was very frightened and threatened," she said. "But if someone who seemed to be so liberal is so afraid, then men who are overt chauvinists must be scared out of their wits."

Moving to the Next Line of Defense

Diane is right about that. While this story has a happy ending, by far the most common reaction that the Samson has when his first line of defense is threatened is to substitute another defense in its place. Some men adopt one of the second-line defense strategies, possessiveness or withdrawal. Others move directly to the more hostile third-line defenses. For still others, the second- or third-line defenses are not a substitute for economic dominance, but an addition to it.

Let's look at the second-line defenses next.

Chapter 5
The Second-Line Defenses: Possessiveness

When Denise Slatick quit her job as head nurse in order to be home with her infant daughter, Jennifer, she abruptly realized that her husband's respect for her took a nose dive. "At first, for a few months after I gave birth to Jenny, Joe was almost in awe of me," she recalls. "It was as if I had performed a minor miracle. But after a while, he seemed to lose respect for me as a person. He rarely listened to what I had to say about anything; he just didn't find hearing about my day or my opinions about anything very interesting. The other thing that happened was that I lost almost all decision-making power in the relationship. Every argument we had about money always ended with him saying, 'When you pay the bills, you can decide how to spend the money.' I couldn't stand it."

Motivated by her husband's attitude, Denise, one year later, returned to work and began experiencing different problems. "It was like I traded in one problem for another," she told us. "Now that I'm back at work, he doesn't hold money over my head anymore. He doesn't ignore me anymore, either. Just the opposite. He's almost gone to the other extreme. He not only listens to me, but he wants a blow-by-blow description of every waking moment I spend away from him. Before, whenever I felt frustrated because he wouldn't give me enough attention, he'd tell me to call a friend if

I needed to talk to someone that badly. Now he resents any time I talk to my friends when he's around. When we're both home, he hangs around me almost constantly. He says it's because he's fallen in love with me all over again and just can't get enough of me." Denise sighed, then added, "To tell you the truth, I feel like I'm being suffocated. I don't know which is worse—his disrespect or this ridiculous possessiveness."

Denise's experience is not uncommon. When economic dominance crumbles or when it never existed, possessiveness frequently becomes the substitute defense. Unable to contain his fear through economic control, the possessive Samson strives at emotional control. In essence he is saying, "If I can't keep you from leaving me or from showing me up by holding the purse strings, I'll control you by holding the emotional strings."

Sometimes possessiveness as a defense emerges slowly, with flashes of jealousy almost imperceptible at first. Other times, it breaks through the minute a woman begins living a life of her own—taking a job, becoming involved in politics, friendships, a hobby—the minute her actions say, "I love you, but I do not live entirely for you." In the case of the more-fearful Samson, it occurs side by side with economic dominance. "I had a patient whose husband tried to totally isolate her from the outside world," one therapist told us. "He built her this immense house in a very remote area of the country. He provided her with every luxury. At the same time, he wouldn't teach her how to drive. He didn't want her to have any close friends. From the outside, it looked as if she were living like a queen, but the fact was that she was really a prisoner."

Whether possessiveness emerges in conjunction with economic dominance or when it crumbles, possessiveness is a potent response to potent fear.

We all experience jealousy and possessiveness from time to time, particularly when someone we love focuses his or her attention elsewhere. But a Samson's possessiveness is different because it is totally out of proportion to the danger. As Karen Horney described it, "It is dictated by a constant fear of losing possession of the person or of his love; consequently any other interest that person may have is a potential danger. . . . Any affection which must be shared with other persons or interests is immediately and entirely devalued."[1]

The Samson who uses possessiveness as a defense is not unlike the prizefighter who gets into trouble in the ring and feels his strength and dominance slipping away. The fighter often defends himself by clutching his opponent, by "holding on." Similarly, a Samson protects himself by holding on to his woman for dear life. Sometimes his fear compels him to hold on so tightly that he squeezes the life out of the relationship.

Like economic dominance, the goal of possessiveness is control: of the woman, of the relationship, and ultimately of the fear, the fear that if he lets go, the woman will leave and be independent of him or that she will prove herself equal or superior to him. Possessiveness strives to control psychologically and emotionally rather than economically. Deep down, the possessive Samson attempts to defend himself by making the woman in his life as dependent on him as he is on her, to turn her into a kind of psychological hostage, to make her feel she can't get along without him.

Possessiveness and Inferiority

Occasionally, the origin of possessiveness is fear of inferiority. When this is the case, a Samson tries to make the woman who threatens him feel as if she cannot function without him unless he's right by her side.

On the job, this kind of possessiveness can often be seen in the male mentor–female protégé relationships, with the mentor becoming angry every time his protégé has an independent thought or when she does things without consulting him first. One woman, for example, told us that the professor who was helping her with her doctoral dissertation recently blew up when he learned that she had asked another professor for advice on how she should approach her topic. "To make a long story short, he told me that I was to come to him first; that I wasn't to consult with other professors without his permission. He also told me that if I wasn't willing to abide by that order, I would have to find another adviser. It was as if he didn't want me to learn anything that he might not know, to doubt him in any way." Eventually, she admitted, she got tired of being "his" student, as he used to put it, and she found herself another, less-cloistering adviser.

Another woman named Betsy told us a similar story with a slightly different bent. "When, after years of being a full-time homemaker and mother, I told my husband that I wanted to open up a catering business, he didn't take it very seriously. His attitude was, 'If you need to have a little something to fill up your spare time, then go ahead.' But the business was no sooner started, when he suddenly decided that he wanted to get more involved. Actually, what he said was, 'You supervise the cooking, and I'll take care of all the rest.' And he did. He virtually took over everything but the cooking. He took care of the books. He handled all the money matters. He set up a computer system for me. And whenever I'd ask him to explain what he was doing, he'd say, 'You don't need to worry about that. I've taken care of it.' It never occurred to me at the time that he worked so hard for the business because he didn't want me to be successful on my own. I thought he was being supportive of me, but what he was really doing was trying to keep me tied to him."

That realization hit when, after fifteen years of marriage, Betsy learned that her husband was having an affair with a younger woman. "I was devastated. I told him that I was going to leave him. Then he asked how I was planning on supporting myself, and of course I told him I'd continue the business. At which point he sort of chuckled and said, 'You know how to cook, but you don't know a goddamned thing about running the business.' And he was right! I had been financially dependent on him before the business, and now I was dependent on him to keep the business going. That's when it dawned on me that the main reason he supported the business was because he was the one who was controlling it." And, as we have said, controlling her at the same time.

Possessiveness and the Fear of Abandonment

Although possessiveness sometimes results from a fear of inferiority, it is more often a fear of rejection and abandonment that triggers possessiveness. In this instance, a Samson's possessiveness comes out as a fierce jealousy toward anything or anyone that takes his one and only away from him. His standard line is "I want you all to myself because I love you so much." In truth, he wants her all to himself because he is extremely dependent on her; he is utterly jealous of anything or anyone that threatens to either expose that dependency or keep him from receiving the all-encompassing attention he demands.

On an unconscious level, the possessive Samson is often looking for the unconditional devotion he wanted but never received from his mother, his first love. We're not saying that mothers do not love their sons, but many mothers, reacting to society's expectations for males, think it's important to push their sons away from them earlier than their daughters. That push often comes before the boy feels ready for it, before he is prepared to be more independent. There is also the frequent dynamic of Dad standing in the way: a boy may come in a close second, but he never forgets that he is second when it comes to Mom's love and·attention.

As a result, many men feel an unquenchable need for unconditional love. Coupled with this need is also a tremendous fear of being abandoned or being pushed away. Behind the possessive Samson, there is often a little boy who is still looking for Mommy's unconditional love and who is scared to death of not getting it.

The search can be endless and consuming; the demands stifling; the jealousy paranoid.

Targets of Men's Jealousy

Other Men—Off Limits

The most obvious target of a Samson's jealous possessiveness is other men. Viewing all of the interaction his woman has with other men as a subconscious slap in the face, a Samson will often try to cut his woman off from having any sort of relationship at all with a member of the opposite sex. Commonly, he will insist that she give up any male friends that she had before they were married, even if they had been long-term platonic relationships or even if the men themselves are married. He badgers her relentlessly with interrogations about the men with whom she works, questioning her incessantly about whom she spoke to on the phone or had lunch with, often demanding a recapitulation of every word exchanged. "I feel like I'm living through the Inquisition," one woman said. "I'm a stockbroker, so of course I work with men. But that's what it is—strictly work. And you know what? I think my husband believes me; I think he knows that I wouldn't cheat on him. Still, I can't help but feel like I'm being interrogated when he asks me questions like, 'What did you talk to John about today?' and I'll say, 'Just the usual business,' and he'll say, 'I bet he made a pass at you.' When I tell him that's ridiculous, he just goes on and on, and then when I refuse to discuss it anymore he'll say, 'Aha! I knew you had something to hide!' It really gets quite insane."

Women—More of a Threat Than Men

Another man isn't the only thing that incites the possessive Samson's jealousy. In fact, men's jealousy of women's female friends is as potent, if not more potent, than their jealousy of men. One homemaker, for instance, told us that her husband had an irritating "habit" of interfering with her phone conversations whenever she was talking with a female friend. "I'll be on the phone when all of a sudden my husband appears in the kitchen. Sometimes he pretends that he's making himself something to eat. Other times, he'll ask me who I'm talking to, and when I tell him, he'll try to wheedle his way into the conversation. Like, if it's my friend Meryl, he'll say 'Oh, tell Meryl hi' or 'How's her husband' or 'Ask her if she's gotten that leak in her basement fixed yet.' There have even been times when I've caught him listening in on the other side of the door."

Nor is men's jealousy of friendships between women confined to the hours that he is home and that he feels she should "rightly" spend with him. In truth, men are jealous of women's friendships, period. One man in an open marriage admitted on a late-night talk show that he was more jealous when his wife spent the day with one of her girlfriends than when she slept with another man. Paraphrasing, his words were something like this: "When she's with another man, I know the kind of intimacy she's experiencing. It's the kind that I can share with her, too. But the intimacy that women have with other women, well, that's something that's frankly out of my range of experience of understanding."

This man is far from alone. On some level, men suspect that women are often more intimate with one another than they are with men. And their intuition is actually right on target. In Eva Margolies's book, *The Best of Friends, the Worst of Enemies: Women's Hidden Power Over Women*, the point that women are frequently more attached to other women than to the men in their lives is documented many times.[2] Even among married women, the trend is evident. When one researcher asked a number of women to name the three people they enjoyed spending time with, only half the women included husbands on their list of three, but ninety-eight percent of them mentioned a woman friend![3] Another study indicated that over half of all married women don't even consider their husbands their best friend![4]

The reasons for this male-female intimacy gap are partly psychological and partly social. The first person that almost every woman is closely attached to is another woman, her mother. The desire to duplicate that early intimacy with another woman remains a staple of feminine psychological development. The fact that males are trained to cauterize their emotions also widens the chasm: it is very difficult to be intimate with someone who doesn't know how to be intimate.

In addition to their fear that women get more emotional nourishment from other women than from men, and the resulting implication that emotionally women don't need men very much, men have also been afraid that if women become too close to each other, they will band together and challenge men's economic and social supremacy. That is why, according to Marilyn French, men throughout history have often tried to destroy women's connection to each other. "Breaking this core," writes Marilyn French in *Beyond Power*, was "essential to asserting male superiority or supremacy. . . . By fragmenting the family social unit of women and denying them the opportunity to form a broader-based political unit . . . they were unable to . . . unify in such a way as to gain power for themselves or to challenge unified male power."[5]

What has been true historically is just as true, or perhaps even truer, today. "I recently joined a women's support group," one woman said, "and my husband has been really up in arms about it. He doesn't understand why I love the group so much, and he is always putting it down. One night I tried to explain the whole idea of sisterhood to him, and you know what he said? 'If your goal is to become one of those bra-burning, women's libber types, you're with the wrong man.' "

Whatever the cause, the upshot is the same: a man is often more jealous of his wife relating to women than men. Given the social and psychological backdrop, it is hardly surprising.

A Samson's Jealousy of Work

The third common target of the possessive Samson's jealousy is a woman's work. For example, he may not mind the fact that she works as long as "Mommy" is there to take care of him and pay attention to him when he gets home. And if she is not? One woman, a nurse, told us that her husband had no objection to her working—as long as her schedule coincided with his. "There was no problem at all when I worked the day shift, because when Barry came home, I was there, too," she told us. But when she accepted a promotion to head nurse that required that she work the 11 P.M.-to-8 A.M. shift, all hell broke loose. "At first, he just got really angry and would throw what I call an adult temper tantrum. When that didn't work, he sort of regressed, you know, became like a little boy. He'd whine that I never spend enough time with him, or would mope for hours on end. I couldn't believe a grown man could act like such a baby." That's because she did not understand that behind her husband's I'm-all-grown-up veneer, there was a possessive little boy who wanted Mommy at home tending to his needs exclusively.

Other women report similar experiences. "I have a very time-consuming career," one public relations executive told us, "and it's true that I'm often involved in something that has to do with work. I frequently have breakfast with people or a drink with someone after work. It's part of my job. He knew all this before we got married, though, and it didn't seem to bother him then. But now that we're man and wife, he complains every time that he happens to be at home and I'm not, even though I spend virtually all of my nonworking hours with him. He says he feels abandoned. He also complains that my work has turned me into a hardnosed businessy type. Yet one of the reasons he said he married me was because I was so competent.

"The strange thing is," she continued, "that he's even busier than I am. He's extremely ambitious careerwise, so there are a lot of times that I am home and he's not. I've pointed that out to him, but it hasn't made any difference. He just has this thing that I should be home whenever he is. I don't know what's come over him or how to deal with it."

What has "come over him" is his dependency on her. As much

as a man might boast that he didn't want to marry or that "she chased me until she finally caught me," unconsciously he often hopes that once he marries, his fantasy of possessing his mother completely will come true. That is why he may suddenly do an about-face in his attitude toward his wife's work. The outside world takes her attention, and Mommy's attention is supposed to be given exclusively to him.

Possessiveness and Objectification

Regardless of whether the possessive Samson is single or married or whether the target of his possessiveness is Delilah's career, her hobbies, or her friends, the same, classic defense mechanism that he is using is called *objectification*. A possessive Samson views the woman in his life less as a person than as an object—someone to whom he can attach himself in order to fulfill his own needs, regardless of how much his neediness depletes her. When she fails to fulfill his needs, his fear can propel him into a paranoid jealousy.

Sometimes a man like this may out-and-out forbid his lover to spend any significant amount of time away from him; should she go against his wishes, he can become quite punitive. "A few weeks ago, the man that I live with told me that he had made plans for us to go away for the weekend," one twenty-nine-year-old cosmetologist told us. "I was angry that he hadn't consulted me. Besides that, it was a good friend's birthday, and I had already made plans to go to dinner and a show with her. He told me to cancel my plans, but I refused. For two weeks, he made my life absolutely miserable. He was downright hostile."

He may also become disparaging. "My husband always has a way of putting my women friends down," admitted Jane, a forty-year-old mother and homemaker. "If they're beautiful, he treats them like sex objects. If they're not very attractive, he refers to them as 'those lesbian friends of yours.' Either way, it makes me feel resentful."

Not surprisingly, the woman on the receiving end of this "Do as I say, I am your lord and master" possessiveness often feels as if she is being choked to death; her response is usually to dredge up every excuse in the book to get away from her Samson and find some breathing space. But more often than not, at the same time that a Samson is being restrictive, he is also sending another powerful message: "I love you so much, I can't live without you. I adore you so that I cannot bear to have you away from me at all."

It is a lure baited with honey. Possessiveness is an effective defense because, for many women, the flattery and the feeling of being idolized may temporarily—and sometimes permanently—blind her to the fact that she is slowly losing her freedom. And often, by the time a woman understands what is really happening, by the time she sees her mate's unrelenting devotion to her as the defense against fear that it really is, her partner has often succeeded in making her so dependent that it is very difficult for her to break free.

The Cloistering of Anne Redding

Meeting Anne Redding, you would never guess that she tolerated the cocoon that her ex-husband Andre kept her in for three years. She is poised and self-assured. She has been successful not at one but at three professions. She moved into her own apartment at twenty and lived alone quite happily for nine years.

"I never waited for a man to come and rescue me," she said. "I guess that's because I could never really count on either of my parents. My mother was an invalid, and my father was rarely around. So at a very young age, I realized that if there was something that needed to be done, I was the one who was going to have to do it."

Yet as Anne was later forced to realize, underneath the armor of self-sufficiency was something else: a yearning, a longing so powerful that during the course of marriage, Anne allowed herself to live as if she were a possession of her husband. During that time, she almost lost many of her friends. Even worse, she nearly lost herself.

In tracing her story, we begin not with her ex-husband but with her three-year live-in relationship with a man named Hal. Hal was very much like the withdrawing Samson we will discuss in the next chapter: interesting, although sexually and emotionally distant; seemingly committed to Anne, but not committed enough to marry her. Unlike Andre, Hal was not jealous or possessive at all.

"We lived together for three years and had a lot of great times," Anne recalled. "And he was very good about giving me freedom— too good, I think. In that relationship, I was always the jealous one. I was the one who was trying to put the brakes on him. I was the one who wanted to get married." But she knew that a pro- posal would never come. "At some point, I realized that Hal was never going to marry me," she said, then added defensively, "and quite honestly, I don't know if I would have married him. I mean, who wants to marry someone they feel they have to beg for love?"

Anne *was* sure, however, that she wanted to get married. "I was thirty-two years old, I had never been married, and it was defi- nitely a priority on my list." She paused, then shook her head as if she had caught herself in a lie. "Actually, it was more than a priority. I wanted someone to love and someone to love me. I was tired of being given the run-around by Hal. I guess the best way to describe my state of mind at the time is 'desperate.' "

Anne's panic was short-lived, for just at the point of greatest panic, her Prince Charming came into her life. "He was handsome and smart. He was independently wealthy and also successful in his own right. He was everything I'd always dreamed of in a man." Her voice dropped. "That's only what I wanted to see, quite hon- estly. I mean, he *was* all those things, but I didn't want to see the other side of the coin."

Who could blame her? Andre was almost the antithesis of Hal. Hal held her love at bay; Andre confessed he was madly in love with Anne on their first date. Hal hedged at commitment; Andre couldn't make one fast enough. "Within a week of meeting me, he told me that he had had a conversation with his sister and had told her that he was going to marry me. Well, that was music to my ears."

From that point on, Anne's *raison d'être* was to please Andre. She went out with him for the first time on a Wednesday; by that Saturday, he had insisted that she move out of Hal's apartment. By the next Monday, she had admitted to Hal that she had met someone else, and she began packing her bags. She stayed with a girlfriend in the interim, speaking to her newly beloved, who lived in Chicago, every day. And then, three weeks later, she left her job, her boyfriend, her apartment, "my life," as she put it, and moved from Boston to Chicago. She was, in her own words, "hooked."

"I had never been involved with anybody who said they were going to call at seven and actually called five minutes early. That's the kind of person Andre was. He gave me this incredible sense of security. He made me feel pretty. He made me feel smart. He made me feel wanted in a way that no one else ever had."

Many years later, Anne was able to understand that all this attention was a sign less of love and devotion than of fear. "The reason he was doing all of this was that he was insecure himself. I later realized that a person who is capable of giving as much as he gave, which was an unnatural amount, does it because of their own insecurities. And they expect an unnatural kind of total devotion in return."[6]

With the help of therapy, she also came to understand the part she had played in Andre's possessiveness. "A part of me rebelled against Andre's jealousy, but an even bigger part of me felt flattered by it. More than that, I wanted to be taken care of. I wanted to be totally intertwined with someone else. On some level, I wanted to be possessed as much as Andre wanted to possess me. I allowed it to happen."

She is quite right. According to Pat Brown, a family therapist in Vermont, it takes the consent of both parties to become involved in an unhealthy relationship. "It's not conscious, of course," she told us, "but there nevertheless is a silent contract between the two parties in which they implicitly agree to remain at a certain stage of development. In this case, both partners were agreeing to remain at a very early, symbiotic stage—a stage at which each is completely dependent on the other. They could have gone on like that forever, as long as both agreed to abide by the contract." As we shall shortly see, Anne eventually reached the point where she was no longer willing to agree. Over time, she came to realize that the kind of love that Andre offered and that a part of her craved came with a steep price tag: her sense of self.

Still, for the moment, the devotion was wonderful. "He put me on a pedestal. He catered to me. He made me breakfast in bed. He made dinner for me. He bought incredible bouquets of flowers for me. He did all of these wonderful things, things that I thought only happened in fairy tales."

But the bliss was short-lived. The fairy tale began to turn into a nightmare at her wedding reception, when Andre did not want Anne to dance with a very dear male friend whom she had known since grade school. Nor did Andre react fondly when, after the honeymoon, they would visit other couples and Anne wanted to be around the men. "He didn't want me to so much as even talk to another man," she said.

Not only were men off limits, but as Anne soon realized, Andre didn't want her to see her women friends either. "It's not that he would actually forbid me," she said, "but I quickly learned that if I went against his wishes, I was going to get grief over it later. For instance, for a while I played racquetball with a woman who lived in our neighborhood, even though Andre didn't want me to. But he made me feel so uptight, I couldn't enjoy myself. I always had the same kind of feeling I used to have when I was a child living at home. If I was fifteen minutes late, my mother would be hanging out the window. So when I was away from Andre doing something I wanted to do, I would become very anxious. I knew that if I didn't get home on time, I'd be yelled at. I didn't feel that I could just call home and say, 'Look, I'm going to be an hour late.' I couldn't reason with him."

It was the threat of that grief, of being punished, coupled with Andre's continuous devotion, that slowly turned Anne from an independent woman into an object of her husband's need; from a woman who knew her own mind to a childlike person who had to tiptoe around in order to avoid raising her "parents' " hackles. Before her marriage, Anne's dress had been flamboyant; conservative Andre wanted her to dress "preppie." Anne was a natural extrovert and had no qualms about doing things like asking other patrons in a restaurant what they were eating and if they enjoyed it. Andre insisted that she "stop talking to strangers." She would go on a business trip to Boston, and if someone would say goodbye to her at the airport, which indicated that she had been talking to someone on the ride, Andre would, as Anne put it, "get nuts." "He didn't want me to have friends, male or female. My old friends were a threat to him. My family was a threat to him. Anything that in any way reminded him that I wasn't born the day he met me was a threat to him."

. So was anything that Anne could do herself. "I actually had to fight with him to let me do the household accounting. I'd always liked being on top of the money situation. I was used to paying the bills." Finally, Andre gave in, and for months Anne balanced the checkbook perfectly. "But one afternoon I was stuck—I had made an error, and I couldn't find it. So I asked Andre to help, and he spotted the trouble right away." She shook her head. "It was a silly mistake, and Andre didn't yell. What he did say was, 'See how much you need me? What would you ever do without me?' It sounds like just a little thing, the way he talked to me, but things like that happened again and again. Over time, I began questioning if I could do anything without him." A message, we might add, that Andre reinforced constantly.

In their work life, the scenario was pretty much the same. Andre owned a sporting goods store in Chicago, and after he and Anne married, they opened two more together. It was a way, Andre said, that they could "eat together, sleep together, and work together." But as soon as Anne, to whom Andre paid a salary, began to take initiative in running the business, to show her competence, Andre's zeal for working did a complete about-face. "He was very bright and very handsome and all the things I said before. Unfortunately, he was the only person that didn't know it. He's a wonderful businessman, a great salesperson. He was very, very charming. But he didn't know that on a core level. So what happened was, the more initiative I took, the more competent I seemed, the less interested in the businesses he became." Then came the bombshell. "After we came home after work one night, Andre announced that he was selling the stores. His excuse was that he wanted to spend all of his time with me. He said that the business was taking up too much of our time. He wanted to spend every waking hour with me."

In retrospect, Anne realizes that Andre's decision to sell the stores and "drop out" was largely wrought out of fear. "I know now that he just didn't want me to think that I could be competent at anything, that I could do anything without him. I had been a very able person before our marriage, and he didn't want me to recognize that because he was afraid he might lose me or that I might show him up." But at the time, all she was aware of was her own fear, her own sense of powerlessness. "I was furious about the stores, but I said nothing. I guess I had reached the point where I believed that I couldn't move without him, breathe without him, live without him. He had me believing that if I left him, I would never be able to find a job. He told me repeatedly that my life before him amounted to nothing. He made me think that nobody else was ever going to love me the way he did, and of course, he was right."

At this point in the interview, Anne had a powerful insight. "I think that if anything had happened to me, if I had been disabled, forced to live in a wheelchair, he would have loved it. After I left him, I finally realized that his mother was an invalid, and I guess what he was trying to do was make me like his mother. He felt most needed when I was in trouble," that is, when she was as dependent on him as he was on her, which she had, in essence, become. "The worst part about it was that even then I didn't realize the full implications of what had happened. Actually, I had to be shocked into realizing who and what I had become."

That shock came a few months after Andre sold the stores, when he decided that they would move to a small town in New Mexico. "It was like a second honeymoon," Anne remembered. "We were all alone, which was perfect for Andre, and he was his usual self, fawning on me, loving me. And since we hadn't met any people yet, there was nothing to fight about."

The lull was broken one night when Anne went to answer the phone, and Andre picked up the extension at the same time. "Hi, babe, is now a good time to talk?" said the male on the other end. "I told the guy he had gotten the wrong number, but the next minute, Andre came into the bedroom, threw down the phone, and pinned me to the bed. He looked really savage and made all these accusations. He didn't hit me, but I was afraid that he might. He wouldn't let me up."

Propelled by fear, Andre had moved into the more vicious third-line defense strategies.

When he finally did let her go, Anne headed for the door. "I was absolutely terrified. He had never done anything like that before." Andre overtook her and grabbed the car keys out of her hand. It was then that the dependence, the helplessness truly hit. "I'm sure that on some level I had resented Andre's control from the start. But it wasn't until that night, alone in the boondocks, far away from everything and everybody, that I realized just how out of control I really was. I was in the middle of nowhere; I had no one to call. And I thought, 'If I can just get a taxi to take me to Albuquerque, I can get on the next plane.' Then I realized that around there you couldn't get a taxi after nine o'clock at night. There were no buses, no trains. I was totally helpless, at Andre's mercy."

Just then, something broke inside her. "I knew that I couldn't continue to live with Andre, that I had to get out. So there I was, alone in the bedroom, but instead of crying or getting depressed, I began making lists . . . what charge accounts needed to be changed back to my name; how to get my share of the money out of the bank; where I was going to live when I moved out. I wasn't one hundred percent ready to leave, but I knew that all the times I had let Andre have his way, all the times I had kowtowed to his demands, had put me in a very vulnerable place. Things had to change."

The next step, although Anne did not consciously realize it, was for her to try a trial separation, to see if she still had enough of the old Anne inside her, to test whether she had become as dependent on Andre as she feared. "We had been fighting again about my spending some time with my friends, but that night Andre did not take away the car keys," Anne recalls. "I had had it, so I packed my dog and my favorite possessions and put them in the car just in case I didn't come back again. I drove until I found a motel that would allow me and my dog to stay, and checked in with my company credit card. I called my old friends; I went out for a drink; I thought about the future and what I wanted to do. I really enjoyed myself. I didn't feel in the least bit lonely."

The next day she went shopping, took herself out to eat, and went to a movie. She was having a "grand old time." That night she called home.

"Andre wanted to know where I was. He was very upset. But I felt like he was getting what he deserved. I guess I wanted to frighten him, because up until that point I had really let him rule me."

Andre pleaded with Anne to come back, and the next day Anne went home. But something within her had changed. "For a few weeks, things were fine. Andre apologized, and we were 'in love again.' But then one night Andre started putting up a fuss about my driving into town for an aerobics class, and all hell broke loose inside me. I screamed like a banshee. I think he thought I had gone off the deep end, and that I was never going to come back," she said. "The funny thing about it was that after that he changed—

for the first time in our relationship, he stopped preventing me from having my own life."

Actually, it's not funny or surprising at all. Time and time again, women told us that as soon as they asserted themselves, when they put their foot down, their partners backed down. And for good reason. Above all, a man like Andre is desperately afraid of being rejected and abandoned. Once it becomes clear that his possessiveness is leading to just that, he very well may decide to cope more directly with his fear rather than deal with the blow of losing the one he loves and the one he depends on so much.

Unfortunately, and this too is often the case, it was too late. The relationship was too scarred. Anne felt like a slave set free, and all she wanted to do was to get away from her oppressor. In fact, only when she no longer felt imprisoned did she realize how imprisoned she had felt. "The more Andre stopped interfering with my life, the more he let me do what I wanted, the more I realized how unhappy I had been, how suffocated I had felt. Anyway, I took a trip back East and spent ten days with my old girlfriend. We talked and talked, and the more we talked, the more I realized that I didn't want to be with Andre anymore. I knew that he was trying to change, but I guess I was afraid that at some point he'd revert back to his old pattern. I also had a tremendous reservoir of resentment toward him. So I called Andre—I guess I was still too afraid to confront him directly—and told him that I was going to get in touch with my lawyer and have him draw up divorce papers."

Andre reverted to his old self. "You'll never leave," he told Anne snidely.

"I believe that he really didn't think I could do it," Anne said. "He didn't think I could survive by myself. He forgot that before I met him I took care of myself. I managed my own life."

Only when Anne came home for her belongings did Andre finally take her seriously, and he begged her to reconsider. "I will do everything, anything for you," he said through muffled sobs.

Anne was in no frame of mind to console him. "You've already done too much for me," she said. "That's the problem."

There were few tears and no loneliness for Anne after she left, only a tremendous feeling of relief. "I felt like I had just been let out of prison. I didn't feel any emptiness. I didn't feel any loneliness. The first morning in my own apartment again, I felt like I did after I had left my mother's house. One of the things I remember clearly is that I woke up and saw that there were no dirty dishes in the sink. It was so nice! I realized that I didn't have to be responsible to someone else anymore, that I didn't have to live for someone else anymore, that I didn't have to listen to someone else anymore."

Today, with the advantage of hindsight, Anne can speculate about how she got locked into such a destructive relationship. "We had such a roller-coaster love affair," she said with an air of objectivity. "It's probably the most intense love I'll ever have. When I left, he told me that I would probably never meet anybody who would love me as much, and he's probably right." But that kind of love, a love that is built on fear as much as on devotion, has, as Anne learned, a high price tag—too high.

"He loved me the wrong way. He loved me as if I were some kind of *thing*, a possession, not a person. He loved me not for what I was but for who he wanted me to be." And what Andre wanted was someone to whom he could parasitically attach himself, someone with whom he could merge.

Of course, it takes two to tango; a woman cannot be possessed by a man unless she allows it. "A lot of it was my fault," Anne admits. Yet even now, it all doesn't quite make sense. "Part of it was that I didn't want to admit that my marriage was failing, which to me meant that I was somehow unlovable, that there was something wrong with me."

There was something else, too. "Andre kept reminding me that there was no one in the world who would ever love me as much as he did. And I must say, he often did make me feel good. He made me feel pretty. He made me feel that if he loved me as much as he did, then I must have some worth."

Anne had been hooked, mind, body, and soul. And she is not unusual. From a very early age, women are taught to base their self-esteem not on their own capabilities but on how much someone else, particularly a man, loves them. That's what makes possessiveness as a defense against men's fear so effective—it plays right into a woman's most profound needs—wanting to be loved and valued. It works with a woman who feels that without a man, she is worthless, that she is nothing.

On the positive side, Anne learned a great deal from her experience. "Andre taught me an incredible lesson. He taught me that you lose someone when you hold on too tight. He also taught me that no one is worth giving up yourself for."

Andre, in his own way, has also benefited. "Since our divorce, he's grown a lot. He's been in therapy and is starting to realize his insecurity, his fear, that led him to be so clutching. When he came to see me last time, he told me that he used to think that trust meant 'Read my mind, do exactly what I want you to do, and then I will trust you.' He realizes now that that isn't what trust is. He's also able to see how unhappy he made me, and has apologized. I believe that he is really sorry."

The contrition, Anne acknowledges sadly, for the first time being able to feel his pain, has another motivation. "He would love a reconciliation," says Anne, "but it's absolutely out of the question. We had dinner twice in the three years that we have been divorced, we have kept in touch, but I'm not the same person anymore. My needs are very different. I won't compromise anymore, not to the extent I did last time. A little compromising is necessary, but I'm not going to give up my friends ever again. I'm also not going to give up my life. I am not going to feel the pressure of having to get home early from work, because my job is just as important as anybody else's. To me, it's more important. So the next relationship I enter will be much more of a partnership. It has to be equally balanced."

To that she adds, "I'm willing to be alone if I can't find what I want."

Many women aren't. Raised on nurturance, a woman's need to be loved often overshadows her need to be her own person. "One of my friends who is married thinks that I'm being too inflexible, that my requirements for a relationship are too high," Anne told us. "But as long as I'm willing to see the other side of the coin, which means there may never be anybody permanent in my life, I think it's my decision to make. It's not like I'm complaining that there is nobody in my life. If somebody comes along who is strong enough to deal with me, to allow the *me* to exist within the *we* situation, great. And if no one like that comes along, it's okay."

We believe her. Having reconstructed her life, Anne now feels content. But every person, man or woman, has a need for what psychologist Andras Angyal calls "homonomy," the feeling of being important to someone else.[7] Unfortunately, Anne came away from her experience feeling that a woman's need for belonging may clash directly with her need for autonomy or independence and that when it comes to having a relationship with a man, a woman can have love or independence but not both.

But multitudes of women are choosing to remain single or are initiating divorce. The inability to integrate love and autonomy hurts women, and at the same time, it confirms men's worst fear: that women can get along quite well without them.

Chapter 6
The Second-Line Defenses: Withdrawal

Every night, Rudy Hines, a twenty-eight-year-old construction worker, comes home, heads straight for the shower, and then watches the evening news while his wife, Dawn, prepares dinner. During the supper hour, as his wife tells him about the trials and tribulations of her day at home with their two children, he develops a chronic case of the yawns. When she asks him about his day, he feeds her his standard line: "I come home to get away from work, not to relive it." Occasionally, Dawn admits, Rudy is a little more attentive—a surefire signal that he wants sex that night. Summarizing her relationship with her husband is simple for Dawn: "He is here in body, and that's about it."

Darrell Rodriguez, on the other hand, isn't even home much in body. As the head of his own successful lock manufacturing company, he could easily hire more help. He insists to his wife, Erika, however, that his physical presence at the firm is the mainstay of his success. To Darrell, Saturday is like every other twelve-hour workday, and Sunday is a day to fizzle out completely. Ask Darrell about his relationship with his nine-month-old son, and he says, "To tell you the truth, I don't really know him. By the time I get home at night, he's usually asleep." Not surprisingly, his wife has similar sentiments toward Darrell. "At this point, our relationship is about as intimate as one between roommates."

Unlike Rudy and Darrell, Stanley Uhl is a single man who has just been, in his own words, "dumped by a woman." For Stanley, being dumped was a shock: in the past it had been he who was the dumper, he who held the upper hand in his relationships with women. "I'm sort of a Don Juan," he says with unabashed pride. Inquire into his feelings about being the "dumpee" for a change, and he offers an insouciant shrug. "It's no big deal," he says. "After all, she's just a woman." You cannot miss the emphasis on the word *just*.

These men vary in age, occupation, and marital status, but they all have one thing in common: all hide their compelling fear of women by keeping emotionally distant from them. Men like this unconsciously build a psychological barricade between themselves and women, denying their fear of inferiority or their own over-powering need for dependence in one heartfelt swoop. Their un-spoken motto is, "If I don't need women, women cannot hurt me."[1]

In extreme cases of withdrawal, a man avoids intimate liaisons with women completely. But a man does not have to go into com-plete seclusion to withdraw. All he has to do is to become out-wardly independent of women or emotionally detached so that women cannot "get" to him emotionally.[2] While he often does not flee physically, he isn't really there.

Withdrawal is generally a much stronger second-line defense than possessiveness. The possessive Samson blockades his fear by hang-ing on, by trying to make himself indispensable. Although not re-sponding in a healthy way, he is nevertheless capable of expressing both his need to be needed and his need to need. He may alienate the woman in his life in the process, as Andre Redding did in Chapter 5, but he does not deny his need for her. A woman may resent being cloistered, but at the same time she also feels wanted and needed by the man in her life. This, in and of itself, is likely to arouse some sympathy and caring on her part.

The man who uses withdrawal as a line of defense against fear is a lot more out of touch. He runs away from both his desire to be loved and his need to love. He does not recognize his phobic fear of rejection and abandonment. He chokes off his emotional side, neither giving nor asking for much in the way of true love. Emotionally defended or, more accurately, blockaded, he feels safe.

Ironically, behind the bravado of the "I can get along without you, you're not to be taken seriously" veneer is usually a man who has a dire fear of his own dependence—and hence of abandonment. In fact, the Samson who leans toward withdrawal as a primary defense usually has tremendous unresolved dependency needs that stem from a less-than-loving mother-son relationship early in his life. Perhaps, in an attempt to push her son into "masculinity," she pushed him away from her before he was ready. Or maybe she simply could not relate to boys. Whatever the cause, the result is that her son didn't get the feeling of unconditional love that he needs before he can break away securely. He left his mother's arms, as he must, but remains dependent at heart—so much so that he fears that if he submits to that dependence he will become totally helpless. This is why he needs to remain detached and uninvolved.

Another kind of mother-son scenario that leads to withdrawal later in life is the overly dominating mother. In this case, a boy's mother is so domineering that he feels that the only way he can establish a separate sense of self, the only way he can break free of her, is to stay clear of women emotionally. As one man with such a mother put it, "Whenever I get too close to a woman, I feel like I'm slowly being suffocated."

Men who use withdrawal as a defense feel, often unconsciously, that they need to detach themselves from women for their own safety. The sad part is that, as we shall shortly see, they often end up emotionally starved.

Three symptoms are characteristic of the withdrawing Samson: emotional distancing; a mechanistic attitude toward sex; and a panic reaction when he feels he is getting too close.

Emotional Distancing

Compared with women, *most* men seem emotionally distant. That's because women are raised to be emotional and to form close attachments, while men are trained to be separate and independent. Men also need to give up their more "feminine" qualities in the name of becoming "masculine." Girls are supposed to be like their mothers. Boys, on the other hand, must not only break away from their mothers, but become different from them: in the process of detaching from Mom, a boy must give up not only his mother, but also all those traits associated with her. The end result is that there are few men who relate with the same kind of expressive emotionalism that women have. Not surprisingly, women often feel that they communicate at cross-purposes with men or that men just don't speak the same language.

The emotional wall surrounding the withdrawing Samson is different from the normal male-female communication gap. The man who does not fear women may not always understand them, but he very much wants to. He is aware of his own nurturing impulses, his "feminine" side (although he may have trouble expressing it). And he easily admits that he is emotionally dependent on them. The withdrawing Samson, on the other hand, finds it difficult to make such an admission, even to himself. If he needs women, it is because they are expedient: they are good cooks, housekeepers, childrearers—boosts to his career. If he admits that he is dependent on a woman emotionally, it is usually with the attitude that he could get along without her, too.

Physically, the withdrawing Samson often isn't around much, either. Rather than spending quality time with a woman, he retreats from her—into his work or his union meetings or his Sunday golf game or his nights out with the boys. When he is there, he frequently uses alcohol or TV as an escape. Psychoanalyst Karen Horney refers to these ploys as "narcotization," a method of waylaying fear by drowning oneself in drugs, drink, or activity.[3]

The withdrawing Samson's fear of being abandoned by women, and the emotional and physical distance that he keeps from them as a result, makes it difficult for this type of man to respond to his woman's emotional needs. Often, he is so out of touch with her feelings that her happiness seems to make little difference to him.[4]

Emotional Distancing and the Single Samson

In the case of the single Samson, emotional distancing has a somewhat different bent. He may, like his counterpart who is married or in a relationship, keep an emotional wall between himself and the woman in his life. But he also commonly sets up standards for women that are so high that he might not be able to find one who lives up to his fantasies.

"I have incredibly high expectations of women," one successful single man told us. "Before I get involved with a woman, she has to have at least fifteen of the twenty features that are important to me. It's sort of a mental checklist that I measure her against, a test, if you will. It includes all kinds of things: what they look like—I can't stand overweight women—to what their home life is like. I look into her background: where she grew up; how she feels about her father. I feel more comfortable with a woman who loves her father than with one who does not have a good relationship with him. I look at her social life—how does she like spending her time? Also her home life—I like to see her home, what she has surrounding her. Does she like being at home? How does she feel about being at home alone? I also like a woman to be strong but not too aggressive. Anyway, if a woman doesn't measure up to my standards, I don't go out with her for long."

Another man expressed similar sentiments. "I've noticed that the women I tend to ask out are inaccessible or undesirable for one reason or another," one man admitted. "Either they are married, or they have something about them that turns me off. For instance, a lot of the women friends I have are bright and strong, but they are also fat, and that turns me off. I also find that the women I gravitate toward are women that challenge me, that awe me, but women like that also tend to be overly aggressive, which is a quality I can't deal with. It's as if I go after women that I can't have, or women I don't really want." His voice drops a key. "Ultimately, I find something wrong with every woman I go out with."

By setting up no-win situations, it's no wonder that men like these have found only a handful of women with whom they have had relationships lasting longer than a few months. Afraid to get too close for fear that their overwhelming dependence will be exposed, they remain blockaded in self-perpetuating isolation.

Somewhat less common is the single Samson who employs withdrawal and economic dominance simultaneously. A man like this bases his entire way of relating to women on his economic achievements. Almost always, he is high-powered and makes a considerable amount of money. In fact, money often substitutes for women as a love object. Attaching himself to possessions is his way of warding off his hidden need for and dependency on women.[5]

A portrait of this type of man was depicted in a recent article in *The New York Times Sunday Magazine*. He is a big spender, mostly on himself, and comes across as being entirely independent of everyone and everything. He also uses his financial leverage as a bait to lure women into superficial relationships. As one of the men interviewed boasted proudly, he only needed to spend five minutes a week arranging his social life. His underlying message was, "Why do I need to spend more than that on women? The whole world wants to date me!"[6]

Although this article was entitled "A Feminist's View of the New Man," the defenses that these men used are as old as men's need to defend themselves against their fear of women. Indeed, if there is anything new about this "new" man, it is that he is more frightened, more vulnerable, and more defensive than ever before.

Distancing and Inferiority

Although the precipitating factor behind emotional distancing is most often fear of abandonment, there are some Samsons who withdraw as a way of defending themselves against their fear of inferiority. Rather than face their own insecurity, they convince themselves that women are not to be taken seriously, and that therefore they are not to be feared.[7]

A man suffering from this fear will avoid any competitive endeavor that he might lose to a woman. And if he can't avoid it, he tells himself that women are incompetent and that therefore any task in which they are involved is not of any real significance: it doesn't matter if he wins or loses. On the job, this is often reflected in the attitude of a man who, when working with an equally qualified or more competent woman, devotes himself less than wholeheartedly to the task. Afraid of being shown up professionally, he convinces himself that "this isn't really important, therefore I need not put my all into it," thereby defusing his fear. So what if a woman performs better than he at a task that is so silly, so meaningless?[8] He is like the child who says defensively, "Who cares that I lost? I didn't even try to win. And the game is dumb, anyway." If he denies that there is any competition or claims that the competition is over something that doesn't matter, how can he be shown to be inferior?

In intimate relationships, his response is very much the same. He will only play games that he knows he can win. He will try to limit conversations to areas of his own expertise. And in cases where his fear is particularly strong and the woman particularly competent, he may pull away completely. "When my husband and I first got married, we were both freelance musicians," one woman told us. "But after a time, I started getting a lot more jobs than he did, largely because I play the cello and he plays the tuba—there are a lot more openings for cellists than tuba players. I think he's a better musician than I am, but that doesn't seem to make any difference to him. He feels really threatened. It's reached the point where every time I talk about a job, he changes the subject. He's even considering changing professions—he says the music business is all bullshit. He's put a wall between us. To tell you the truth, I'm not sure if the relationship is going to make it.

"The worst part," she added, "is that I can't understand why he feels the way he does. We have other friends, mostly male, who are musicians and who have been getting more jobs than he has for years. That never seemed to bother him."

We are not surprised. For a man to lose out to another man is to be expected from time to time. For a man to lose out to a woman strikes at the heart of his shaky sense of his own masculinity, at the heart of his fear.

It is no wonder that single women who are professionally successful have so much difficulty finding a man. "I have been very successful in my career," a woman named Marcia told us, "but when it comes to men, I've been a total loss. They are completely intimidated by my success. My apartment is filled with expensive art, and it's furnished beautifully. But most men I go out with for the first time take one look at how I live, how well I've done, and they're ready to head straight out the door. It's gotten to the point that when I first go out with a man, I meet him on neutral territory. But then, of course, he wants to see my home, and almost always, that's the end of that. Somehow, they feel as if they have to compete with me." And one suspects that they feel that they might lose.

A Mechanistic Attitude Toward Sex

Another characteristic of the withdrawing Samson is that he often separates sex from emotion. For both men and women, intercourse can be an emotionally charged experience. But for a man, particularly an emotionally needy Samson, an intimate sexual experience often has a certain edge because it more closely evokes the feeling of fusion and closeness he once had with his mother. These feelings are frightening because they often reawaken the unconscious dependence and helplessness that he once felt with his mother as a boy; these are feelings that the withdrawing Samson tries to defend himself against by keeping his emotions in check during lovemaking.

A man like this may be a good lover in that he is sensitive to a woman's sexual needs, but he never completely lets go of himself emotionally in the process. His passion is controlled because he is afraid of being carried away by his feelings.[9] Mentally, he is much more comfortable with the idea of having "great sex" than with "making love." He may say that he loves women, but what he usually means is that he loves their bodies and the pleasure he derives from them.

Frequently, a Samson who separates sex from emotion uses mildly disparaging terms during intercourse, reducing his lover to a kind of object in his own mind. "You're a great piece of ass" is typical of this kind of remark. Labeling her as a thing, he keeps his dependence in check. After all, an object does not abandon you, reject you, or make you feel inferior.

The Prostitute-Madonna Syndrome: A Special Case of Withdrawal

When a man's fear of women is particularly strong, he may go so far as to divide women into two distinct categories—the prostitutes and the madonnas—in order to feel safe with them. The madonnas are all those sweet, Doris Day types toward whom he feels love like the love he felt for his mother. Madonnas are not really sexual; nor are they real. Therefore they are not to be feared. And of course sex with them is ultimately safe since such women are viewed as having no great need for sex.

The prostitutes, of course, are another story. They are women that men lust after but usually don't consider marrying. A prostitute is someone who sells services that can be bought with cash; it's strictly a business relationship. And then there are the mistresses men have, women married men have affairs with but never leave their wives for. "I love you, honey," he says to his mistress when she pushes for an emotional commitment, "but I just can't give up my family." What he really means is; "You are just an object to me, and a somewhat tarnished one at that. You are expendable, a pretty thing to be handled and used." By "debasing the object," he keeps himself above it all, in control—safe.

Almost always, the man who splits women in this way has another fear in addition to those of an ordinary Samson: the fear of his own incestuous desires toward his mother. "A man like this has never resolved the Oedipus complex," Angela Fox told us. "That is, he's never transferred his longings toward his mother to other women. And when that happens, sexual relations with women can be really frightening, because they rearouse those old and very forbidden feelings. That's why he has to withdraw sexually from women either by disparaging them or by desexualizing them."

The Panic at Closeness

Another characteristic of the withdrawing Samson is his tendency to flee when a relationship gets too close. A man like this wants nothing more than to be loved by a woman, but his fear of abandonment makes the experience of intimate love too risky. The result is that just as he feels himself getting too involved, too dependent, too close, he retreats emotionally into his shell.

"It makes no sense to me," one woman told us, speaking of her husband. "Every once in a while, Ken and I will have a very intimate moment where we really bare our souls, our innermost thoughts and feelings. I always feel terrific when something like that happens, as if our relationship has taken another step forward. But I've noticed that whenever we share such intimate moments, Ken suddenly becomes distant. It's almost as if he wished that he could take back whatever he's told me. He becomes really cold toward me; detached, in a way. It's as if for every step forward we take in our relationship, we take two steps back."

Another way of pulling back is to have a series of short-term affairs. Behind almost every Don Juan exists a man who is both terribly dependent on women and terrified of that dependence. "It's a way of escaping," Dr. Jane Flax, a practicing psychotherapist in Washington D.C., told us. "These flings are usually very intense at the outset, but once the relationship begins to take hold, there's total panic. That's because the man is looking for a feeling of fusion with a woman, but he has to flee from it before it takes over, before he feels really stuck."

A similar dynamic underlies the need of many married men to have one-night stands. Men like these are usually very much in love with their wives, and they experience a fair amount of guilt about their trysts. At the same time, their need to prove to themselves their independence from their wives overrides their desire to remain loyal. As one man put it, "Having sexual experiences with a number of women that I will never see again is how I keep a certain amount of space between me and my wife. It's really my way of saying that I am in control of our relationship, that I am in charge, that I am not completely dependent on my wife for everything."

This man is far more in touch than most. Most often, even when a Samson is aware of his approach-avoidance reaction to closeness, he is usually oblivious to its roots. "I've noticed that I tend to chase women who are a little standoffish, who play a little hard to get," one twenty-nine-year-old bachelor confessed. "I'll really go all out trying to win her heart: sending flowers, writing little romantic notes—the whole bit. The thing is that once the woman starts to show signs that she cares, once she sends the message, 'Okay, you've won me over,' I lose interest. The blush is lost. The romance fades."

Ask him why he thinks that happens, and an expression of genuine perplexity crosses his face. "I've dwelled on this for many drunken hours, and the only thing I can think of is that I am afraid of women 'getting me.' That's why my relationships require that I'm in the driver's seat, that I'm the one in control." Yet on some level this man knows just how tenuous that control is, which is why once the intimacy begins, it's his signal to move on. Karen Horney wrote that people of this type run away from love because to fall in love "would mean losing control and letting themselves be carried into unknown territory."[10]

How Withdrawal Controls

What is so compelling about withdrawal is its effectiveness as a defense. Psychologically, withdrawal allows a man to hide his fears behind the guise of his independence from women. What gives withdrawal a particularly strong edge, however, is that it gives a man a tremendous amount of control over the woman in his life as well.

Emotional distancing is an insidious way for a man to keep a hold over a woman because it breeds insecurity in the woman who experiences it. A withdrawing Samson comes across as being "above it all" when it comes to expressing his feelings for a woman, giving her the distinct feeling that she is not really needed, that she is readily replaceable. Never sure of her position, she strives to be all he wants her to be in order to keep what little affection he gives. The omnipresent possibility of rejection hangs over her like a dark cloud, and it can threaten to turn her into an emotional lapdog. She does what he wants her to do, devouring the few scraps of love that he throws to her from time to time.

If the relationship is extended over time, it often becomes an emotional roller coaster for the woman. As described by one thirty-two-year-old woman who has been waiting for a proposal from the man she has been seeing for three years, the process goes something like this: "The thing that first attracted me to Sandy was that he was so gentle and attentive to me when we first met. He was very considerate, a lot of fun, and seemed very open about his feelings. I had never met a man that I hit it off so well with, and within a few months I felt myself getting very involved with him emotionally. One night I told him that I thought I was falling in love with him, and he said he thought he loved me, too. The trouble started after that. A week later he said that he wasn't really ready to make a commitment to me, and that he wanted to see other women. At first I just stayed home waiting for him to run back to me, but when he continued to date other women, I decided to date other men. He got really upset when he found out about that. He dropped the other women he was seeing, told me how much he loved me, but said he wasn't quite ready for marriage. I didn't want to pressure him, so I told him there was no hurry. I was also hooked on him again; he was caring and loving the way he was when we first became involved. Anyway, a few months later, he started having to work late all the time—at least, that's what he said. But then I found out he was seeing someone else. I was really furious and told him I didn't want to see him again. That lasted for two weeks, and then he came back begging my forgiveness. I took him back and then a few months after that, he reverted to his old inconsiderate self."

This "I love you, I love you not" routine has been going on for three painful years. "I just keep believing that someday he'll come around," she said. "The thing is that when things are good between us they are very good. I just can't seem to break up with him as long as there is hope." Nor is she able to put her foot down and demand a commitment. "I guess I'm afraid that if I tell him that I really need a commitment from him, he'll break up with me for good."

While this woman still has a chance to break free of this man's hold, life is not so easy for the already married, particularly if a woman has children and no means of financial support. "My husband spends more time with his buddies than he does with me," one wife complained. "Sure, I'm resentful, but what am I supposed to do? If I bother him about it, he just complains that I'm a nag, and I end up getting less from him than before."

A person who seems to be in such control can also be very frightening. He often appears to be like a walking time bomb— you're never quite sure when he is going to go off. "I have this feeling that behind my husband's reserved exterior, there is a walking volcano," one woman confessed. "And that scares me, because he's six feet one and I'm five feet two. So in a way, I'm always on my guard. . . . I never want to incite him because I'm not really sure of what would happen if his emotions all came out."

Finally, someone who comes across as "above it all" or "detached from it all" can be very intimidating to be around. That's because he gives off the message that he is certain of himself, unruffled, and therefore superior. Writing about her father, author Signe Hammer put it well: "He maintains dominance easily, since there is the force of so much emotion behind his control. Women respect him, since his control says, over and over again, 'I am superior to you—I keep my cool.' "[11]

The sad part about all this cool and control is that the man who defends against his fear of women by withdrawing from them hurts himself in the long run even more than he hurts women. By keeping women at arm's length, he denies not only a woman's emotional needs but his own needs as well. He puts himself in an emotional prison. Deep down, he desperately needs affection from a woman, but his actions preclude him from giving and hence from getting the love that he needs. This leaves him in a deadly psychological Catch-22: he needs to be close to a woman, but he cannot be intimate with one.

The Noncommittal Male—Withdrawal as a First-Line Defense

This double bind was most poignantly seen in the single men we interviewed who could not make a long-term commitment to a woman. For these men, withdrawal substituted for economic dominance as a first-line defense. Yet while withdrawal defended them against their fear of abandonment, most were very unhappy. They often admitted to being quite lonely, yet for reasons they did not usually understand, they just couldn't seem to make a relationship with a woman work. They felt the need to always be in control in their relationships, but many could not help but feel the isolation, the bondage of their own loneliness.

In our interviews, we found that the most common psychic scenario behind men who could not make commitments to women was a rejecting mother and a rejection by another woman at a critical juncture in his development, often during adolescence. The combination of the two experiences left these men terribly needy emotionally, but they were so afraid of further rejection that they could not get what they needed.

A few of these Samsons, often with the help of therapy, were able to break free of the fetters of their earlier rejections. But others, like the man in the following story, seem potentially wounded for life.

When Dick Gibbons first spelled out the parameters of his childhood, nothing seemed particularly unusual. He was raised in a middle-class Catholic family, the fifth of six children, the youngest of three sons. His father was a teacher, his mother a housewife. He'll tell you that his life was mostly okay—not enough money sometimes, but mostly okay.

But ask him to talk about his mother, and his expression changes.

He becomes fidgety. The pitch of his voice rises ever so slightly. Occasionally a glimmer of seething hostility flashes across his face, then, quickly controlled, it burns behind his eyes.

Calmly, he says that he and his mother didn't really have a bad relationship, just not much of a relationship. She was harried by her many children. Deep down, he suspects that had his mother believed in birth control, he would never have been conceived.

He also knows that Mom did not have any great love of sons. In fact, what he remembers most about growing up with Mom was that she fawned all over "the girls," who were pretty and obedient, while complaining about the other three "rowdy hellions." "She couldn't relate to boys," he says. "She was always frowning on typical male behavior." The corners of his mouth turn down almost imperceptibly. "To this day, she prefers my sisters."

If you look closely, you can almost see the hurt. But ask Dick directly about how his mother's rejection affected him, and a wall goes up. "My mother was not a very bright woman," he responds, "and I began tuning her out very early. Her effect on me was insignificant."

It's difficult to communicate to a man like Dick that there is no such thing as an "insignificant" rejection by the first woman in his life; that his attempt to minimize the potency of that rejection is the first line of defense in his "women don't matter much" veneer. He is not purposely lying, but rather he is unconsciously trying to protect himself from the hurt. Men who feel rejected by their mothers have to hide their feelings of hurt behind so many emotional layers that they frequently become out of touch with the source of the original damage: the feelings of anger and abandonment that arise from being rejected. Listening to Dick Gibbons's story, we suspect that the damage was considerable.

"When a boy is rejected by his mother, the effect can be devastating," Angela Fox told us. "It makes him feel insecure not only in his mother's love but in the love of all women. Even if he is loved by a woman later in life, he can't really trust that love because deep down he feels that he isn't really lovable."

What made things so much worse for Dick was that in addition to being rejected for himself, he was also rejected for his maleness. That's the ultimate slap to a little boy's masculinity: the ultimate rejection by the most important woman in his life.

As Dick grew older, his mother's disdain for male "rowdiness" was replaced by contempt for male sexuality. "As I said, my mother was a devout Catholic. Anyway, I think I was about twelve or so. I had just discovered masturbation. Anyway, one night my mother came into my room and caught me—well, kind of—I was under the covers. She gave me such an incredible look of disgust that I didn't touch myself for a month afterward."

It also, he told us, made him anxious about his sexual feelings toward girls when he reached adolescence. Sigmund Freud was the first to point out that a man's anxiety about sexual relations with women arises from the fact that it's usually his mother who first places prohibitions on his sexuality. This ban makes the boy angry, an anger that is suppressed because of his overwhelming need for his mother. It is that need, coupled with a feeling of rejection, that leaves behind a residue of fear.[12] "I remember feeling very shy, almost frightened of girls when I was a teenager," Dick recalled. "I always felt that my mother was looking over my shoulder every time I even thought about kissing a girl. She made me feel that my sexuality was a bad thing, something dirty. I didn't even kiss a girl until I was almost seventeen."

That girl was Katie Simmons, and she was gorgeous. She also pursued Dick with starry-eyed idolization. "The way I first found out that she liked me was that one of her friends told me that she thought I was a hunk," Dick said, smiling. "I liked that. It made me feel like a real man." It also made him feel that it was good to *be* a man.

Dick and Katie began dating at the end of their junior year, and from their first date on, Dick was obsessed with thoughts of her. He thought about her endlessly. Katie was beautiful. Katie was kind and caring. Katie understood him like no one else did. Not seeing her for a day or two felt intolerable. "She was everything I could have wanted in a girl," he said. He might have added, she was everything he wanted but did not get from his mother, too.

Of course, Dick Gibbons is not alone in this knockout type of first love. Many boys experience it. During adolescence, a boy's sexual and emotional feelings, which up until then center on Mom, need to be displaced. Girlfriends become safe replacements for the arms of the mother the boy must leave.

But for a boy who does not feel loved or accepted by his mother, for a boy like Dick Gibbons, the experience of first love has an added edge. Not having had the experience of being loved by his mother that every boy needs to develop in a healthy way, the craving for love is that much more urgent in him. Thus, when and if rejection hits, which in the throes of adolescent love it almost inevitably does, the blow is that much more devastating.

In their senior year, Katie and Dick began sleeping together. For him, sex was not the "conquest" that many of the other boys boasted about. "I never spoke about my sexual relationship with Katie with any of the guys. In fact, I never really spoke to anyone except Katie about much of anything. My whole life revolved around her. Sex just made me feel that much more strongly attached to her. It made me feel as if she really loved me. I wanted to marry her."

If Katie *had* married Dick, chances are he could have turned his mother's rejection from an open wound into a nonpainful scar. He may have had a tendency toward overpossessiveness, perhaps, but he would have been able to give love and get it.

Unfortunately, what was for Dick the end of a search for love was for Katie only the beginning; what could have healed his rejection by his mother ended up reinforcing it.

Disaster struck the night of their senior prom. Dick had known that Katie was going to school out of town, but until then he had, without asking, been certain that she would remain faithful to him. After all, they had talked about plans for him to visit her on weekends. But Katie had other plans.

On the beach where they had driven to escape the crowd, Dick protected Katie's bare arms from the cool breeze. "God, Katie, do you really have to go away?" Dick said, nuzzling her hair.

Katie's body arched as if in pain.

"I love you, Dick," she said, "but I've been feeling that things are moving too quickly for me. I mean, I'm only eighteen."

"Look, I'm not going to pressure you to get married," he said implacably, concealing his mounting anxiety and trying to take control of both the conversation and himself. "We can wait until we're out of college if that's what you want."

Then came the blow. "What I mean is that I'm not sure if you're the one I want to marry. You're the only guy I've dated steadily, and I just don't feel ready to make a permanent commitment. So when I'm at school, I'd like to see you, but I'd also like to go out with other guys, too."

Dick became blind with rage. "I wanted to smash her face in, to tear her apart, literally," Dick recalled. "That's all I remember."

His original rejection by his mother replayed with a different face, Dick withdrew from women almost completely for four years. Occasionally during college he'd "get laid," as he put it, but most of his leisure time was spent getting smashed with his fraternity brothers. And the girls he did date were mostly high schoolers, girls who looked up to him, girls with whom he indisputably had the upper hand. "After Katie, my whole attitude toward women changed. I didn't trust them, didn't want to take a chance with them. Other than sex, I frankly had no need for them." What he was really saying, of course, was that he needed women desperately, yet he was too afraid of not being needed in return, too afraid of being rejected. That unconscious fear still influences his life.

Dick is thirty-one now, but on some levels he is still the young man who was rejected at eighteen and the son who was rejected as a child. He dates a little more, has even had one relationship that lasted almost a year, but that ended because "I'm not interested in making a serious commitment." He is vaguely aware of sometimes leading women on emotionally, only to drop them when they fall in love with him. Vaguely, he is aware of this need-to-punish power play. Karen Horney traced this attitude to the mother, "by whom he felt humiliated and whom he wished to humiliate in return."[13] But insight has done little to ease the pain: for the most part, Dick has become a hardened and sad man, a man who is as much a victim of the Samson and Delilah Complex as a perpetuator of it.

"I'll never let a woman get to me again," he says with a false air of pride that barely hides the anger underneath. For in this statement, he is writing not only a script of hurt and maltreatment for every woman who tries to "get to him" but the script of his own inevitable loneliness as well.

Women also have a rough time when they are rejected by their first love. They, too, can be afraid, but the injury is usually less severe, and it heals faster. For men, as one study noted, the loss of the first adult relationship "throws them into a turmoil and depression of the most extreme kind."[14] In his practice, Freud saw the same thing: men who lost their first love often withdrew to the point that they were unable to seek out new relationships. Women, on the other hand, tended not to retreat to the same degree and were more able to look elsewhere for new relationships.[15] The reason for this discrepancy goes back to the taproot of men's fear: men rely on women emotionally more than women rely on men. And when they allow that dependence to surface, only to be rejected or abandoned, the hurt is shattering.

Withdrawal + Economic Dominance = Intimate Strangers

Of course, not every Samson's fear is so strong that he feels compelled to dodge women completely. For men who can make a long-term commitment to a woman but who are frightened enough that they need to keep some emotional distance from her, different scenarios develop. These are the men who marry but who pull back emotionally as soon as their own dependence begins to show itself. These are the men so many wives complain about: men who seem emotionally backward, who seem only halfheartedly committed to their relationships; men who seem to be married more to their leisure activities or to their jobs than to their wives.

While the noncommittal Samson is usually aware, on some level, of his fear of women, the fear and dependence of a Samson who marries and then withdraws often remains hidden until after he's crossed the threshold. He may brag that it was she who chased him and finally "got" him, but with each passing year, he cannot help but note his increasing need for her. He feels it often in small ways at first—hurt and rejection when she does not smile at him; jealousy of his own children when she seems more attentive to them than to him; a twinge of desolation when he longs for her but she has her own agenda to attend to. Whatever the source, he must confront the extent and depth of his need for her. When he makes that recognition, he retreats, struggling blindly against his own neediness as he tries to protect himself from anything that even faintly resembles the dependence that he fears so much.[16]

This flight into withdrawal occasionally occurs by itself as a second line of defense, but we found that it is often used by men who are simultaneously defending themselves using economic dominance. The combination of the two defenses can be deadly to a marriage, breeding distance, turning lovers into intimate strangers.

In the early stages of such relationships, it's usually the woman who suffers most, who feels emotionally betrayed. But if the couple is together for an extended period of time, it's usually the man who ends up bearing the brunt of his own withdrawal. That's because, when a man reaches midlife, he frequently feels a need to reassess his life, and more time with wife and family is often high on his new list of priorities. After years of affirmation that his spouse is not going to abandon him, he begins to mellow out, to shed his fear. The tragedy is that by this time his children already think of him as a stranger, and his wife has already created her own life—a life apart from his.

Women and the Withdrawing Samson

At this point, an important question must be asked: What kind of woman would opt to stay with a withdrawing Samson?

Sometimes she herself has a problem with intimacy or dependence. "I've had a number of patients who are continuously attracted to men who are afraid of intimacy," Angela Fox told us. "For example, there was one woman who, for years, would choose men who weren't interested in making any sort of commitment." Her attitude was, 'If I have to win this person, then it's better, more valuable than if the love comes easily,' which of course was her own neurotic defense against commitment. For a woman like this, the man who is elusive is perfect, because she always is able to maintain her distance, to never get involved."

More often, however, she is economically dependent, believing that her life would be a financial struggle without her Samson's income. She forgoes her need for an intimate relationship in exchange for financial security.

Interestingly, even a woman who is not economically dependent on a man may come to perceive herself that way, particularly when the man in her life earns a lot more money than she does. One woman who earned $50,000 a year admitted to putting up with a withdrawing Samson for four years because over the course of their relationship she had become accustomed to a quality of life that she herself could not have afforded. He belonged to old-money society. He had a country house overlooking the beach, and he took her skiing in the French Alps over Christmas vacation. True, he kept her waiting all the time. True, she always felt that she had to "push" her way into his life. But breaking up with him also meant giving up a lifestyle that she could never have afforded on her own.

Whether her economic dependence is real or perceived, such a woman feels stuck. But even dependents grow up and mature, and many women, when faced with a withdrawing Samson, begin making plans for their forays into the working world, which is often the first step in moving out of the relationship. Not surprisingly, when this happens, a Samson becomes that much more threatened and often moves into the vicious third line of defense.

Chapter 7

The Third-Line Defenses: Physical Violence, Humiliation, and Sabotage

Tracy Michaelson is a woman who, for seven years, passively deferred to her husband Gabe's every wish, to the point of almost complete subservience. Gabe allowed Tracy almost no freedom. He was adamantly against her working, and he refused even to discuss the matter. The large salary he brought in was completely under his control. Like a child, Tracy went to Gabe each week for her allowance, and Gabe made her account for every nickel she spent. Nor was Tracy allowed to go out with her friends without Gabe's permission, permission that was frequently denied. Paradoxically, Gabe himself was rarely home. When he wasn't on the road selling insurance, he was out gallivanting with his buddies at the local bar. Tracy had complained early in their relationship about what she viewed as a double standard, but her "nagging" only made Gabe more distant. Gabe was a combination Samson—economically dominant, possessive, and withdrawn—but Tracy was financially and emotionally dependent on him. So she did things his way in order to keep the peace.

Tracy's docile servitude suddenly stopped a year ago. "Something just snapped" is how she explained it. "For years, my mother had been telling me that I was a fool to let Gabe control me the way he did, and finally I realized that she was right. I decided I wasn't going to put up with it anymore, but I also knew that that meant I would have to find a way to support myself." After seeing a vocational counselor, Tracy decided to enroll in a training program to become a physical therapist.

Gabe surprised Tracy with his initial reaction to her plan. "He was amazingly calm about the whole thing. His only stipulations were that I take care of any child-care arrangements and that I keep the household running. I say 'only' because I was expecting an out-and-out explosion."

What at first looked like acquiescence, however, quickly showed itself to be disbelief in disguise: Gabe just did not really believe that Tracy was going to stick it out. When Tracy's mother came for a visit, for example, she asked Gabe what he thought of her new career plans. "You mean those courses she's taking?" he sniggered. "Surely you don't think she's really serious about finishing. I haven't known Tracy to finish any project she's started."

It was true. Since Gabe had known her, Tracy had been big on plans but even bigger on procrastination. But Tracy was growing, changing. After completing her first year, it became stunningly evident that never-finish-anything Tracy was a person of the past. The person who replaced her was more assertive, independent, and goal-oriented.

As the new Tracy emerged, so did a new, malicious Gabe. The hostility was relentless. What used to be occasional put-downs became a regular part of Gabe's interaction with his wife. When Tracy responded by ignoring him, he became verbally abusive, throwing every derogatory name in the book at her, often in the presence of their children. Gabe refused to talk about her classes, and when she discussed her progress when they had company, Gabe would yawn and announce that the subject bored him. "Things got so bad that he never had anything positive to say to me. I think he was trying to wear me down with his hostility, but I wasn't going to let him."

Things came to a head one evening when Tracy was on the phone with one of her classmates. Gabe came home, barged into the bedroom where Tracy was talking, and announced that he was hungry.

"I'll be five minutes," Tracy said calmly.

A minute later Gabe returned. "I said I was hungry," he snarled, grabbing the phone out of Tracy's hand and slamming the receiver down.

Tracy glared at Gabe, then picked up her pocketbook. "I'm getting out of here."

Gabe froze, a look of madness clouding his face. Tracy ran out the door and started the car. Gabe suddenly appeared, and before Tracy had time to roll up her windows, Gabe had his hands menacingly around her neck. "He was not really choking me," Tracy said, "but it was obvious that he could have."

Gabe begged Tracy to come back into the house, tears filling his eyes. Frightened, Tracy complied. Once inside, Gabe broke down. "I don't know what got into me," he said between sobs. "I guess I was so afraid that you would leave me. You can't leave, Tracy, you can't. I love you. I promise nothing like this will ever happen again."

Tracy was too stunned to think clearly. But she knew one thing: If Gabe ever laid a hand on her again, she was going to walk out for good. Gabe must have intuited her feelings, because he has not been violent since. That is not to say that the potential is not there. "It has become obvious that Gabe is extremely threatened by my becoming my own person. He still is not supportive of my training, and sometimes I wonder what is going to happen once I finish school and start bringing in a decent income. Will he calm down or become a raving maniac? As far as I can see, it's a fifty-fifty chance of things going in either direction."

Gabe's reactions are not atypical. When the first- and second-line defense strategies are insufficient to hide a man's fear, when they do not adequately keep a woman under his thumb, the more violent and hostile third-line defense strategies come into play.

It is important to emphasize that the third-line defenses do not always sequentially follow the breakdown of the first- and second-line defenses. A possessive Samson, for example, may combine humiliation with his other tactics to effectively restrict a woman's outside activities. If his humiliation of her results in shaking her self-confidence, she is unlikely to pursue any activities that do not include him. In other cases, third-line defenses may occur alone—some men are chronic humiliators, for example. In a work setting, moreover, the first two lines of defense are usually not viable, so a fearful Samson must go directly to third-line defenses. Either way, the man who uses third-line defenses is afraid to the point of total panic. The man who resorts to the third-line defense strategies is a man walking on psychological tenterhooks, a man who is so afraid of losing control that he will stop at almost nothing to keep his fear in check.

Tracy Michaelson's husband Gabe manifested all the classic third-line defenses: humiliation, violence, and sabotage. Alone or in combination, each of these defenses can be an effective means of control—and potentially destructive to the woman who is victimized by them.

Physical Violence

The most frightening of the third-line defenses is physical violence. Women may be equal to men, even superior to them in some ways, but when it comes to physical strength, there's little doubt that men are a lot stronger than women. That is why physical violence often emerges as a defense when a man feels most threatened. It's the one surefire way that he can prove his superiority; it is his last-ditch attempt to exert control.

Physical violence is obviously an intimidation tactic, and the Samson who resorts to such extreme measures is attempting to scare a woman into submission. At its most extreme, there are chronic abusers and men who murder women who won't comply with their wishes or fulfill their needs. But a man does not have to be a wife beater to use his maleness as a method of domination. Of the women that we interviewed, nearly half admitted that at one time or another they had been physically intimidated by a man in their lives.

"My husband has never laid a hand on me," one five-foot-three, one-hundred-fifteen-pound teacher told us. "But when I go against his will, he is often prone to fits of rage. He becomes hostile and verbally abusive. At its worst, he begins breaking up the house, you know, throwing things. He really loses control. My husband is six one and weighs two hundred pounds. He's so big and seems so out of control when he gets like that that I really become frightened. Sometimes I give in just to pacify him."

Other women report similar stories. Although not abused in the classic sense, they told us that, in one way or another, the Samson in their lives had at various times relied on his larger physical size and greater strength to exert control. Some men pushed. Others, like Andre Redding in Chapter 5, physically confined their wives by pinning them down on the bed or by grabbing them and not letting them go. The specifics varied, but the underlying message was always the same: "Do as I say—or else."

If the physically violent Samson is usually the most frightening Samson, he is also usually the most frightened. Beneath the facade of power, there is always a man who feels terrified and powerless, whose panic button has been pushed. Indeed, almost every woman who had encountered a physically violent Samson told us that the violence erupted when she had in one way or another communicated, "You are not the lord and master, you cannot control me," or, as in Tracy Michaelson's case, she made the most fear-provoking communication of all: "You cannot make me stay with you."

Physical Violence and the Breakdown of Economic Dominance

Indeed, the inner dynamics of men who resort to violence in their relationships with women are revealing not only of a particular man's underlying terror but also of a growing fear among men in general. Although we'd like to believe that male violence toward women is on the wane, there are some unnerving indicators that suggest that just the opposite might be occurring given the move toward equality for women.

In the past few months alone, we have noted several newspaper stories in which a man reportedly killed his wife because she decided to get a job against his will. One article in *The Washington Post* indicated that there has been a rise in wife abuse, and it linked this phenomenon to a poor economy.[1] Less extreme but nonetheless telling is the observation that there has been an increase in the number of movies that depict extreme violence against women. In 1983, one out of eight movies depicted violent acts against women, compared with one in twenty just one year earlier. Nor are films such as these safe outlets for men's aggressive impulses. Researchers have found that movies containing violence against women are sexually stimulating to one-third of the men who watch them. There is also evidence that repeated showings of films like these harden men's attitudes toward women, and they may even instill attitudes similar to those of rapists in the minds of viewers.[2] The same trend is emerging in other media. In recent years, for example, some publishers have introduced a new line of "macho" books, replete with tall, imposing men who use their physical strength and prowess to keep women under their thumbs. Sales are climbing.[3]

The New Generation of Samsons: Physical Violence as a First Line of Defense

Are these data reflective of the older generation of Samsons who are on the way out? Hardly. If anything, violence toward women is increasing not in the older sector of the male population but among its younger members. In fact, *among the younger generation of single men, there are indications that physical violence in the form of rape may be the new first line of defense against fear!*

It has long been established that rape is not a crime of passion but of power. And from all indications, young men's need to assert their power over women seems to be escalating. In a three-year survey of 6,500 university students nationwide, preliminary results showed that one out of every eight women had been raped. Nearly half of those women said the rapists were either first dates, casual dates, or romantic acquaintances. A survey conducted at Brown University uncovered similar findings. Sixteen percent of the women reported that they had been forced to have sexual intercourse by men they either knew or were dating. Eleven percent of the men at the university actually admitted to forcing a woman to have intercourse. This newly discovered phenomenon has been given the name "date rape." Its occurrence is so frequent that college campuses across the country are establishing educational programs to alert women to the possibility of such "casual" rape.[4]

If only a small minority of young men actually engage in rape, a significant number of men admit that they might consider raping a woman if there were no consequences. In one recent study, approximately thirty-five percent of male college students admitted that they would probably rape a woman if they could get away with it. Other research has placed the estimate as high as sixty percent. If men could be assured of no punishment, rape would be a common occurrence.[5]

Although it is far from the norm, sexual abuse of women by

young, educated men is on the rise, particularly among fraternity men. In a recent article in *Ms.* magazine, one national executive director of a major fraternity said that the problem "has become epidemic in recent years." The reason, according to Andrew Merton, who authored the article, is clear: "The transition to college represents a first step in a struggle for a kind of 'manhood' from which women are viewed as objects of conquest—worthy, but decidedly inferior, adversaries. The idea of women as equals is strange and inconvenient at best, terrifying at worst."[6]

These findings suggest that today's young men are no less likely to be Samsons than were their predecessors. If anything, as women become increasingly independent, men's fear seems to be getting worse.

Humiliation

Although less threatening in terms of actual physical harm, humiliation is also a virulent form of control. The goals of the Samson who humiliates women are to hide his fears by making women look small and to transform his feelings of "impotence into the experience of omnipotence," as Eric Fromm put it.[7] Deep down, he aims to make the victim of his humiliation feel helpless and insignificant. As long as the woman in his life feels incompetent, how can she possibly be a threat? And if she accepts being the object of his degradation, she never *will* be.

The negative self-image that humiliation reinforces can be devastating. It works the same with adults as with children, where it is most often seen. The youngster who is repeatedly told that he will never amount to anything will fulfill the prophecy: by adulthood, the idea that he is a "loser" is so ingrained that he feels incapable of doing anything worthwhile. The same is true of a woman with a Samson who humiliates her. If he reinforces the idea that she is nothing without him, over time she may perceive this as the truth.

"I was very good friends with a woman in college," a man named Victor told us. "She was very bright and creative. But then she married this awful guy who tried to completely control her life. He was always putting everything she said down, as if she were a birdbrain. Whenever she ventured an opinion on something, he'd tell her that she didn't know enough about the subject to make an intelligent judgment. The worst thing was that she eventually started acting like a birdbrain. I had dinner at their house a few weeks ago after not seeing her for a year, and she barely opened her mouth. And anytime this jerk of a husband talked, she nodded her head in agreement. After dinner, I took her aside and remarked on how quiet she'd been. And she said, 'Well, I'm sure that I wouldn't have anything very interesting to contribute.' "

Most men, from time to time, put women down. The man who never cracks a nasty little joke about the female sex is rare indeed. But while it's true that there is often an element of fear involved in these little asides, an occasional comment about what are perceived to be women's innate frailties does not mean that a man is a Samson.

Indeed, women sometimes say similar things about men. A common complaint among women is that "men are such babies when they're sick." Whether it is voiced to other women or directly to the man involved (often just to provoke an indignant response), a comment like this does not mean that the woman believes men are inferior.

Women frequently hear about stereotypical "locker-room talk"; the all-male locker-room setting creates an atmosphere wherein men can boast of their conquests or put women down. Such talk boosts men's egos and does not necessarily mean they are humiliators, for they don't necessarily mean what they say.

The man who uses humiliation as a defense, however, is another breed completely, for his motives are sadistic. His purpose is to degrade a woman into feeling helpless and powerless, to "put her in her place" or "show her who's boss." In the most benign case, he wants her to feel ridiculous and unworthy; in more extreme instances, he tries to destroy her self-respect.[8]

Anything that the Samson who wants to humiliate thinks will make a woman feel demeaned or inadequate is likely to be a included in his disparaging remarks. He may attack her looks, her personality, or her housekeeping ability, for example, or make fun of her conversations with other women. In Marilyn French's novel *The Women's Room*, traditional homemakers found themselves the objects of their husbands' humiliation. Their husbands considered the women's friends inane, and therefore, by association, their wives were inane, too.

Female Anatomy

Another common target for some Samsons is a woman's sexuality: more specifically, her inability to achieve full sexual release solely through "vaginal" orgasms. A man like this resents and often chides a woman who needs additional clitoral stimulation during intercourse in order to reach orgasm. To him, Masters and Johnson are quacks. "I recently broke up with a man who became out-and-out incensed when I didn't have an orgasm unless my hand or his hand was on my clitoris," one woman said. "Intellectually, I knew that most women were just like me, but emotionally, he made me feel abnormal. Over time, I began to feel like a freak, like there was something wrong with me."

Underneath the "I'm such a wonderful lover, what's wrong with you" veneer, men like this are terribly insecure about their sexuality. It bothers them that women need additional stimulation because it implies that the thrust of their mighty penis is insufficient for complete sexual satisfaction. Men like this often harbor negative feelings about women who masturbate, because implicitly the message is "I don't need you for sexual pleasure. I can do it myself."

Although motivated by fear, the tactic of chiding women for needing clitoral stimulation has been highly successful in achieving its aim—to make a woman feel inadequate. Ask any sex therapist these days what problem women most often come to their offices about, and they're likely to tell you "the inability to have orgasms the 'right way.' " Yet as medical research has repeatedly proved, there is no such thing as a "vaginal" orgasm. The overwhelming majority of women need clitoral stimulation during intercourse in order to reach orgasm. Nor is this need indicative of an innate flaw, as some men have implied. The clitoris is the primary female sex organ, just as the penis is the center of male sexual response. A woman's vagina, like a man's testicles, is a secondary sex organ. Just as most women cannot have an orgasm with only vaginal stimulation, most men would not be able to climax if the only stimulation they got was of the testicles. Men's need to cling to the myth of the vaginal orgasm in the face of overriding evidence to the contrary is clearly a sign of their own feelings of inadequacy. Sadly, many women have not seen men's fear for what it is and have allowed men to use the myth to make them feel sexually inferior—which, of course, is precisely what some men have intended.

Covert Humiliation

A man may humiliate a woman through omission as well as commission. Although the attack is not direct, the woman still feels humiliated. She finds her self-worth diminishing, or she comes to believe that she is not intelligent enough to understand anything. One woman named Andrea told us that she had recently telephoned Fran, the wife of a couple with whom she and her husband frequently socialized. Fran's husband was Andrea's lawyer, and he had just won a claim in Andrea's favor that was worth $40,000. When Fran asked, "How are you?" Andrea replied that she was flying high because of the recent legal victory that Fran's husband had implemented. "I knew nothing about that," Fran confessed to Andrea. "*He* never tells me anything." Andrea breezily brushed it off, saying, "Oh well, maybe he didn't think you'd be interested." Fran sighed. "Oh no, I ask him to tell me things all the time, but he insists they're too complicated. Sometimes it feels like he doesn't think I have a brain."

Similarly, a man may never compliment the woman he is with, yet he may bestow adoring glances on every other woman in the room. Or he may forget to send her flowers or a card on her birthday, but his secretary receives a bouquet on Secretary's Day. Behavior like this makes a woman feel unattractive, inhibited, and insecure, unsure of her value as a person.

Public Humiliation

Although much of men's disparagement of women goes on behind the privacy of closed doors or in all-male contexts like the locker room, the more insecure Samson will often go public with his disparaging remarks. Not only does he need to show the woman in his life who is in charge, he needs to prove it to the world.

We recently witnessed this kind of public put-down when some acquaintances of ours came for brunch. It was during one of those friendly, heated debates that couples often engage in when they get together. The subject was President Reagan's proposed tax reform plan.

Jeff, a bright, successful real estate salesman, thought the proposed elimination of tax deductions for second homes would be disastrous for the economy. "Real estate values, particularly in the large urban areas where there is a lot of co-oping, will take a nose dive," he said emphatically. "There will be very little incentive to invest."

"I disagree," his wife, Rose, replied. "If real estate values drop, more people who could not afford to buy a house or an apartment will be able to."

Jeff waved his hand impatiently, as if dismissing not only the statement but his wife. "Some people always have opinions on things they know nothing about," he said, the expression on his face more a sneer than a smile.

Rose ignored his outburst and continued. "There would be an initial shake-up, of course, and rents would probably rise somewhat—"

Jeff looked at her with open contempt. Then he attacked. "You're not out there working. You don't see what's going on. You don't even read a newspaper! What the hell do you know, anyway?"

Underneath his contempt, of course, he fears that she knows as much as he does, and perhaps more. A man like Jeff disparages a woman in public because when his wife expresses an opinion that's different from his, especially if it's an intelligent opinion, he hears it as a threat, as an assault on his masculinity. His fear compels him to be the big boss, the man in charge. Now that authority is being publicly challenged, he needs to save face, and he does so at her expense.

Of course, rather than sitting silently as Rose did, a woman can defend herself publicly. But after a time, continual disparagement, particularly in front of others, can break one's spirit. That is what makes humiliation so effective as a defense. Nor is the feeling of resignation limited to the dependent homemaker. Even Jeane Kirkpatrick admitted that she did not "bear up very well under it," referring to the public humiliation of being called "Mrs." despite her Ph.D. or of being described as "schoolmarmish" while her male counterparts were called "professorial."[9]

Sabotage

When his fear is sufficiently strong, Samson may become an outright saboteur. Like the Samson who humiliates, the Samson who sabotages aims at breaking a woman's spirit. By throwing a barrage of obstacles in a woman's way, he strives to wear her down, to destroy her confidence and self-respect, and to batter her integrity.

More often than not, sabotage is practiced as a defense against the sense of inferiority that the Samson feels as a result of not achieving enough in the world of work. Despite the changing times, being successful and being in charge on the job is still the equivalent of being masculine. Take away that superiority, and a Samson's self-esteem often comes crashing down. That is why so many men work so hard to make it difficult for women to achieve success and power and prestige. Deep down, they hope that if they make things tough enough, the majority of women will retreat back to the kitchen or drown in the anonymity of the secretarial pool.

Sadly, their strategy is often effective: Samsons in the work world have successfully sabotaged the careers of many women. Newspaper and magazine articles are replete with stories about women who, confronted with obstacles and hurdles every step of the way, eventually give up and drop out. As a woman attorney-turned-mother-and-homemaker put it, "As a woman in a predominantly male profession, I was in the position of constantly having to prove myself. Everyone makes mistakes, but when a woman screws up, it's always because 'she's a woman.' A lot of men I worked with were out-and-out hostile, would do everything they could to intimidate me or make me look bad. Then there were those who don't hurt you, but they don't help you, either. Of course," she added, "there were a few guys who were really supportive, who were secure in themselves and didn't mind competing with a woman. But they were few and far between, and after a while I burned out. I couldn't take it anymore. It's a real zoo out there."

Unfortunately, as many women have learned, things may be just as bad at home, too.

The Sabotaging Spouse

A recent study of husbands married to corporate executives revealed that fifty percent of the men could be considered what the researchers called "subtle obstructionists," [10] that is, men who in one way or another sabotaged their wives' efforts to get ahead. Thus, one out of every two men married to a successful corporate woman is to some extent a sabotaging Samson.

Our interviews confirm this finding. Professional women frequently complained that their husbands, subtly and sometimes not so subtly, put obstacles in the way of their success. Often the sabotage took the form of relentless hostility. "Recently, I accepted a job promotion that required that I travel one weekend a month," a woman named Tanya told us. "My husband is a salesman and travels quite a bit, but when I told him about the job, he had a fit. He didn't want me to take it and told me if I did, not to expect his support. To make a long story short, I took the job over his objections because I didn't think he was being fair. He's made my life miserable since. He's nasty a lot. He used to help with the housework, but no more. Whenever I travel, I come home to an absolute pigpen—dishes piled in the sink, laundry strewn all over the place. He makes me feel totally responsible for the upkeep of the house, in addition to my job, and I resent him for it. He makes me feel like I have to make a choice—my marriage or my success."

Other career women sabotaged by their Samsons found themselves in even more compelling double binds. One attorney put it this way, "When I first met Tony, he always talked about the idea of shared parenthood. He firmly believed in active fathering. But ever since Alice was born, he's changed his tune. He leaves almost all of the childrearing to me. When she gets sick, he expects me to stay home with her. About a month ago, she started running a high fever late at night. The next morning, I had a very important business meeting and didn't feel comfortable leaving her with the sitter. When I asked him to stay home and watch her, he refused and told me that was my job. I started screaming that it was his child, too, to which he said that sick children need their mothers, not their fathers. He wouldn't budge. I ended up staying at home with her all the next week, and my boss was very angry. He said that he'd excuse it this time, but in the future I'd have to make other arrangements because he couldn't afford to count on women who were pulled in two directions. So what do I do? If I leave my sick child, I'm an irresponsible mother. If I stay at home with her, I'm an unreliable worker. Either way, I'm damned.

"It's absolutely incredible," she continued, "how this supposedly liberated man has turned out to be so sexist."

In truth, it is not incredible. As we pointed out earlier, many closet Samsons emerge from the closet once they become fathers. A man can often tolerate a woman's success in their prechild days because he views them as being on equal ground. But the birth of a child destroys that equilibrium. Not only can his wife do what he can do in the world of achievement; now she can do something he cannot: bear children. An unconscious fear of inferiority is triggered, and the man often responds by trying to restore the balance. The move to push her out of "his" world begins.

On the conscious level, the man often becomes jealous of the new child. He is no longer the center of his wife's attention, and he may begin sabotaging her in subtle ways to gain some of her attention. He may interrupt her with "Where's my dinner?" when she's feeding the baby, or he may complain that he has no clean shirts to wear to work but the baby has a closet full of freshly laundered clothing. Instead of gaining his wife's attention in a positive way, he more often than not elicits her annoyance or exasperation. This in turn exacerbates his fears, and he may even step up the sabotage. It's not surprising that even when a woman works and earns as much money as her husband, she still is made to bear most of the homemaking and childrearing responsibility.[11] Even when companies offer paternity leaves, few men take them.[12]

Covert Sabotage

Although most forms of sabotage are overt, there is another form of sabotage that is just as damaging, although it is far less obvious. We call this *covert sabotage* because it does not initially appear to be sabotage at all but rather has many of the elements of breakdown.

Rather than sabotage a woman directly, a Samson who practices covert sabotage falls apart when the woman in his life needs him the most. Looking for support, what she finds instead is someone who needs support himself. She needs his help, but suddenly he becomes a helpless dependent. She wants to direct her efforts toward her own self-development, but his "neediness" forces her to focus her efforts on getting him well. Sometimes she responds by feeling guilty. "If what I'm doing is making him sick, then maybe I should stop" is the message she may tell herself.

Like most defenses, covert sabotage is not conscious. A Samson does not tell himself, "I'm going to get sick so that she'll have to take care of me." But on an unconscious level, that is precisely what his actions are saying.

The Sabotaging Breakdown of Philip M.

The most compelling story we heard about this less-typical form of sabotage came from a woman we shall call Leslie M. The underlying dynamics of their story—her husband Philip's terror as Leslie became increasingly successful, his sabotage of her career in the form of a psychological breakdown—although uncommon, still occur too often.

One atypical aspect of this story is that Philip was not your typical Samson who feared his wife's success from the start. If anything, Philip appeared to be a paragon of the confident, liberated man: supportive, egalitarian, with no need to defend himself at all. In fact, he was the epitome of what we call the *counterphobic* Samson, that is, a man who hides his fear by attaching himself to an ambitious woman just to prove how unafraid he is. But as we shall see, once that counterphobic facade is pierced, the facade may come crashing down.

"If you had told me five years ago that deep down Philip was a man with a hidden fear of inferiority, I would have laughed in your face," said Leslie, who at thirty-seven exudes a quiet confidence. "He would have probably laughed it off, too. To tell you the truth, I honestly don't know who was more surprised by his breakdown, he or I."

Philip and Leslie met ten years ago at a business convention. Philip was a corporate golden boy, on his way to the presidency of his company. Leslie was a secretary who painted as a hobby. It was the painter Philip fell in love with.

"I'll never forget the first time I showed Philip some of my canvases," she told us. "He loved them. He said he couldn't believe that such an exceptionally talented woman was wasting her time as a secretary."

Philip and Leslie fell in love, and they moved in together. Six months later, Philip proposed. "Marry me," he told her. "And then do what you should be doing—painting."

Leslie protested. "You know I can't earn a decent income by painting."

"I know that you should have someone supporting you until you can," he replied.

Leslie felt uncomfortable with the idea. "I don't like to think of myself as dependent," she said squarely.

"All right, then," he answered, "when you're rich and famous, you can pay me back."

"You can see why I never had an inkling that Philip was insecure," Leslie told us. "Frankly, I don't even think he knew it." She's right about that. The counterphobic Samson hides his fear from women, to be sure, but also from himself. The typical Samson covers his fear by trying to control. The counterphobic Samson's defense is the pretense that he has no need to control at all.

The first three years of their marriage were, according to Leslie, like a dream. They had a child that they both adored, and Leslie was free to devote most of her time to developing her talents because Philip's income afforded full-time live-in help. Yet despite the fact that she was doing what she wanted to do, Leslie continued to feel uneasy about her lack of income.

"It really bothered me that I wasn't earning any money," she said. "There were a lot of times that I told Philip I wanted to get a job, that I didn't like the fact that I was dependent on him. But Philip would always talk me out of it, telling me that if I held on a little longer, my big break would come. He seemed convinced that I was going to be a big success."

What Leslie knows now, but didn't know then, was that unconsciously Philip was actually afraid that she might be successful. He liked being her "sponsor" because that meant that she needed him. He needed to be the big breadwinner because underneath his bravado, he had a dire fear of inferiority. Philip seemed to be supporting Leslie the artist, but his support came readily because Leslie was a *struggling* artist. That realization came to Leslie only when she stopped struggling.

On a dreary summer day, Philip, fatigued and sweaty, came home to his ebullient wife. Leslie had been making her rounds to dealers when a customer in one of the art stores had approached her. He was a vice president for one of the country's largest greeting card companies, he explained, and he loved her work.

"I know you're probably into gallery work," he told her, "but if you'd be interested, I'd be happy to offer you a job as an illustrator."

An hour later, Leslie was sitting in the vice president's office. An hour after that, she was hired.

Philip found it difficult to share his wife's enthusiasm. "But, honey, is this really the kind of work you want to do? And the money is so lousy."

He was right. Leslie's starting salary was a meager $18,000 a year—a mere drop in the bucket for someone who had been working to develop her talent for so long.

But Leslie wasn't to be swayed. "It's a start, Philip, a real start."

She took the job, and she loved every minute of it. She frequently worked overtime or brought work home in the evenings, but she did not mind in the least. "I felt like I was blossoming," Leslie said. "It wasn't gallery work, but I found that I enjoyed it almost as much. I also felt that I had tapped an unknown talent. I seemed to have a very good sense from the start about how to communicate the copy I was given into pictures."

Leslie's move up the ranks was swift. Her ideas quickly set a new standard for excellence. She had a flair for dealing with people, too, soothing the nerves and egos of the most difficult clients. Three months after being hired, she was given a 25 percent raise.

At the same time that Leslie was receiving accolades, however, Philip was passed over for a promotion to vice president. The man who was chosen was ten years Philip's junior, and Philip was crushed. He became depressed. But the real problem was yet to show itself.

Six months after Leslie received her first raise, her boss called her into his office. "The creative director is going to another company, and I thought you might like the job."

"I don't know if I'm ready for that," Leslie said honestly. "I haven't been here very long, and it's a very high-pressure position."

"You're right, it is. And it will be difficult at first. But you're very talented, and I know you can do it. Besides, I'm willing to double your salary if you accept."

That night she excitedly told Philip about her raise and promotion. They toasted the great event with expensive champagne.

The next morning, Philip started getting sick.

We say "started" because his "illness" lasted two years. Over these two years, he vomited spontaneously, had migraines, and drank heavily. In the evenings, he'd sit in front of the TV, depressed for hours. Worst of all, he spent money recklessly, putting his family at the edge of bankruptcy.

"It was like living in a nightmare. This man that I had been married to, who I thought I knew so well, just fell apart on me. The pressure was terrible. I had the household to run, my job to take care of, which was getting increasingly demanding, and debtors to ward off. And of course," she added, "now there was Philip to take care of, too."

Philip, Leslie also learned, hadn't been showing up regularly at work. "His boss called me up and told me that Philip had to do something to get his act together. He wasn't performing well when he was there, and some of the time, he didn't even come into work at all."

Leslie insisted Philip see a psychiatrist. It didn't help. "He seemed to get even more depressed," Leslie said, "and I was becoming more and more frightened."

Just how frightened she was and how desperate the situation was became apparent when Leslie called Philip at his hotel when he was purportedly on an out-of-town trip. Philip, she learned, had never shown up. Panic-stricken, she called a close friend.

"I can understand that you're upset,'" her friend offered. "It sounds like he's having an affair."

"An affair!" Leslie screamed hysterically. "I'd be happy if he *were* having an affair. I'm afraid that he's in some locked garage with the car windows shut and the ignition on!"

"I felt so angry, so betrayed," Leslie told us. "Here I was, successful for the first time, going half out of my mind with work responsibilities, and here was my supposedly supportive husband falling apart at the seams. If he had to have a midlife crisis, why then?"

But Philip was not experiencing midlife crisis. Nor was he having a breakdown in the true sense of the word. Unconsciously, Philip *wanted* to be sick. His illness was his defense, his way of sabotaging Leslie's career, his way of hiding his fear of abandonment and inferiority by making Leslie feel sorry for him. It was an example of what psychologist Judith Bardwick calls the "weaker inhibiting the stronger."[13] And the strategy was working.

"I was run ragged," Leslie told us. "I would wake up in the middle of the night sweating. I had acute attacks of anxiety. And I was so distraught and tense all the time that my work began to suffer. It was as if all my creative energy were being drained."

Did Leslie ever consider leaving Philip during that period? we wondered.

"Often. But how can you leave someone when they're so needy?"

Precisely. Although Philip didn't know it then, his illness was his way of making sure that Leslie would remain by his side always, of ensuring that she would never show him up professionally. His demonstration of weakness was his way of saying, "If you love me, you'll quit."

Actually, she didn't have to. Almost two years after Leslie's promotion, her company was bought out, and her whole department got the ax.

Leslie came home in shock and for the entire next week, she stayed in bed. Her depression was agonizing.

Then a curious thing happened. Philip, who had been continuously sick for two years, started to get well. "If I hadn't seen it, I wouldn't have believed it," Leslie said. "He went from being an emotional cripple to his old self within six weeks. He seemed to spontaneously recover."

Confronting the Source of Fear

Such a miraculous "recovery" may sound far-fetched, but this story is true. Nor is such a remission of symptoms as unbelievable or uncommon as one might think. Mental health professionals have known for a long time that psychic distress can vanish, seemingly overnight, when the source of that distress is removed. Remove the fear-triggering situation, and the fear seems to disappear. Of course, only the symptoms—not the fear—really go away.

Philip didn't spontaneously recover at all. Instead the source of

Philip's fear—Leslie's success—was removed, and his need to defend himself through sabotage was gone.

Philip is nevertheless the epitome of the closet Samson, the man whose fear does not show itself until there is an event that triggers that fear. Given the changing social climate in which male chauvinism, a direct manifestation of fear, is increasingly frowned upon, one might suspect that there are quite a few closet Samsons lurking in the background.

A study conducted at Virginia Commonwealth University shows this to be so. Attempting to differentiate sexist from nonsexist men, the researchers gave their male subjects an attitudinal test. Based on the subject's responses, a man was placed in either the sexist or the nonsexist group. Both groups of men were then shown a movie that depicted assertive, liberated women. After the movie, both groups of men were once again given a pen and paper test in order to determine how the movie had affected them. The results were astonishing. Both groups responded with equal hostility to the women in the movie. The researcher's conclusion was telling: to say you're a liberated man is one thing; to be a liberated man is yet another.[14]

Philip's story was typical in that third-line defenses frequently lead a woman to hand down an ultimatum: "Either you change, or I am going to leave." After Philip "recovered" and Leslie overcame her depression, Leslie insisted that they seek counseling. She explained that she just didn't trust Philip anymore, that she really wasn't sure who he was. At first, Philip balked, but Leslie told him she would leave him unless he agreed. The threat of abandonment, the fear that been closeted, was now real. Like many men who are forced to see that controlling their fear by controlling a woman leads only to rejection, Philip gave in.

In counseling, which lasted two years, Philip was able to finally confront his "breakdown" for what it was: an attempt to keep Leslie from showing him up. The fact that Leslie had never earned close to Philip's income made little difference: the threat that someday she *might* earn as much as he, *might* be more successful than he, had been sufficient to panic him. He came to understand his own insecurity about his masculinity, that his ever-present need to be superior did not make much sense or make him happy or make his marriage secure. Most important, he acknowledged how much he needed Leslie and that if he were not able to work through his fear and adapt, he would eventually lose her.

From all appearances, Philip has adapted. Six months into their therapy, Leslie, still without a job, decided to go into her own business. Today, four years later, she is successful beyond her most optimistic hopes, and cards with her art and signature are in shops across the country. The second year into her business, her income matched Philip's. For the past two years, it has surpassed it.

"I'm very proud of Leslie," Philip told us with genuine pride. "It took me a long time to get to a place where I really felt comfortable with the idea of a wife who is as successful or more successful than I am, but I think I'm finally there."

Publicly, Leslie agrees. "Philip is now one of the most supportive husbands I've ever met," she told us in his presence. "We're closer now than we ever have been."

But privately, Leslie admits that despite the years of therapy and the day-to-day proof that Philip has overcome his fear, she still does not completely trust it. "On the outside I seem cool and confident, but the truth is, on the inside I'm a nervous wreck. Sometimes I wake up in the middle of the night sweating with anxiety. I want to believe that Philip's really changed, but there is still this little voice that says, 'What if you make too much money this year, what if you become even more successful? Is Philip going to fall apart on you again?' What happened is now long past. Still, the wounds are not totally gone."

How Women React to Third-Line Defenses

Leslie speaks for many, if not the majority of women who have felt the brunt of the third-line defense strategies, physical violence, humiliation, and sabotage. And for good reason. A man who uses third-line defense strategies is one who has been afraid of women for a long time, perhaps for most of his life. The roots of his fear run so deep that one is wise to realize that it never goes away completely; that his fear may attack him again at some later time. Remission is a real possibility, however, if a man works to achieve it. If a man faces and deals with his fear, he can strive toward a more egalitarian relationship with the woman in his life. More important, most men who work toward overcoming their fear discover to their delight that they are more loved, more appreciated, and more secure in their relationships than they were when anxiety ruled their lives.

Of course, not all men are forced to adjust. Sometimes the women in their lives allow themselves to be controlled by this third line of defense, living with humiliation, sabotage, even violence for years. As we shall see in Part II, the only way a woman can overcome a Samson's defenses is to take the risk of challenging them.

It is a risk, because not all men are capable of adjusting. Some men's fears are so intractable that they cannot overcome them. Often, if a man suspects that his partner is just bluffing, that her discontent is real but that her ability to end the relationship is not, his third-line defenses might be intensified. One farmer's wife had put up with her husband's economic dominance, possessiveness, humiliation, and violent temper for years. Feeling as if she had reached the breaking point, she packed the children into their pickup truck one day and left. However, her flight was temporary. Unable to fend for herself, she went back to him. Frightened by her abandonment, her husband was a changed man for a few months. Then his Samson-like ways started again. His wife threatened to leave, but she did not. With his fear of abandonment now justified and his control over his wife very real, this man became out-and-out abusive.

Another possibility when a man's defenses are broken is flight. "For years, my ex-husband tried to control me," one forty-two-year-old divorcee said. "He was threatened by my independence. It bothered him that I was economically self-sufficient. He was very hostile a lot of the time and made my life miserable. Finally, I put my foot down and told him that while I loved him, I couldn't live that way anymore, that he had to respect my freedom. He said he couldn't do it; he just couldn't deal with my independence. He said it would be easier for him to leave me because eventually he'd get over me, but he could never get over my independence. And that's what he did: he left."

Actually, the man in this example was lucky. At least his wife gave him a chance to reconsider his ways. Unfortunately, the dominating tactics of a Samson can be so hurtful and destructive that by the time a woman musters the courage to leave, she has absolutely no interest in giving the man a chance to adapt. From her point of view, she has been kept captive, a prisoner. When she discovers how to escape her cell, she does not want to turn back. Samson's fear of abandonment has been confirmed. And it is he who has made it come true.

Chapter 8

Breakdown: The Blockade Comes Tumbling Down

Up to this point, we have discussed three primary ways that Samsons deal with women who challenge their defenses. Some men flee, often latching on to a more dependent woman, as did Jim Tiers in Chapter 4. Others put up more defenses in an effort to tighten the controls. Still others, like Philip M., eventually move past their fears and adjust. But what happens when a man cannot flee the source of his fear? Or when he is unable to defend himself against it or constructively deal with it?

At this point, a Samson will experience some sort of physical or mental breakdown. The man who is desperately afraid yet who has been stripped of coping mechanisms to deal with his fear is a man in dire straits. He stands face to face with his fear, confronting the Samson and Delilah Complex head on.

The symptoms of overt breakdown vary from man to man, but most commonly they include one or more of the following:

- depression
- anxiety
- sexual difficulties such as impotence over a period of time
- paranoia
- excessive drinking or drug use that does not quell his anxiety
- the emergence of suicidal tendencies such as reckless driving

- recurring fits of violence that appear to have no apparent cause
- deterioration in job performance
- psychosomatic ailments, including backache, stomach ache, headache, chest pains, hypertension
- utter passivity and compliance

We should emphasize that not every man who experiences a breakdown is aware of the source of his panic. But he does know that he is anxious and frightened and that he has little control over those feelings. He feels desperate, but he does not know where to run or where to hide.

A look at some recent statistics suggests that there are an increasing number of men who, when forced to confront their fear, don't know how to handle it. Mental health practitioners report that as a result of the "new feminism," many more men are suffering from sexual impotence.[1] Male suicide is on the rise, particularly among men between the ages of fifteen and forty-four.[2] Between 1970 and 1980, the overall rate of suicide among men rose from 18 to 20 per 100,000. But among men between the ages of 25 and 34, the rise was from 19.9 to 26.2! Men are also increasingly plagued by serious mental health problems: according to government estimates, the number of men admitted to mental hospitals has increased by about ten percent in the last decade.[3]

Recent news reports indicate that women's rebellion against men's control has created tremendous psychological stress for many men, driving more and more of them into therapy. As one recent article pointed out, men's fear of women "is no more common now than in the past, but it is more problematic. They come to treatment more these days because women are less willing to put up with them." These men feel abandoned when their wives go back to school or work, or they are "insecure about the durability of [their] masculinity" and are threatened by the increase in women's power. Often these men have adopted a strong Samson veneer, a "hypermasculine" posture, as Dr. John Munder Ross calls it, in order to hide their fear, only to find that the posturing no longer works. Just as often, however, they espouse egalitarian values, only to discover that what they say is a far cry from the way they feel. Almost always, they are men who find that their relationships with the women in their lives are floundering.[4]

For some Samsons, overt breakdown precipitates the beginning of true growth. Through therapy or his own soul-searching, a man begins to recognize his fear for what it is and how that fear is detrimental both to his relationships with women and to his own development. Acknowledging his struggle and his genuine effort to change, the woman in his life often will stand by his side and support him through the painstaking process.

But there are many Samsons who resist change, even when they are in the throes of breakdown. The more frightened the Samson, the more he needs to change, but paradoxically, the more Samson-like he is, the more resistant he will be to changing. This leaves him in a terrible bind. He experiences his relationship as being extremely insecure. He knows the woman in his life is becoming intolerant of his Samson-like ways. At the same time, he resists coping with his fear, or he suspects that it will take him so long to change that she will not wait around long enough for him to do so. Given this backdrop, how can he avoid losing her?

Submissiveness as a Covert Form of Breakdown

A number of men, when pushed to this point, become completely submissive to the demands and expectations of the women in their lives. Submissiveness as a covert form of breakdown is a way both to ward off an overt breakdown and to hold on to a failing relationship (or in the case of a woman who has already left, a way of trying to lure her back). The submissive Samson's unconscious thinking goes something like this: "If I do everything she wants, everything she says, maybe she won't leave me; maybe I'll be able to win her back."

It is important to differentiate the man who has always been submissive in his relationships with women from the man who becomes submissive after other defenses have failed. The man who has always been submissive is the henpecked husband, the wimp, who responds to every one of his wife's demands with a compliant "yes, dear." Almost invariably, such a man is the product of a lifelong dependence on a controlling, domineering mother. Afraid of losing his mother's love, and later on, the love of the woman he marries, he does everything in his power to pacify her. Submissiveness is not his last resort, but his first line of defense.

The Samson who becomes submissive only after the other defenses have failed is different, as his submissiveness *is* a last resort. Although the details differ from man to man, the general scenario leading to submissiveness is predictable. Almost always, the submissive Samson is a man who has been put on notice by a woman: "Either you stop your controlling Samson ways immediately, or I'm leaving." His own rigidity and fear are so deeply ingrained that he suspects that he will not be able to work though them quickly enough. What could be a golden opportunity for real growth instead becomes a nightmare characterized by fear of rejection and abandonment. Trapped, he feels he has no recourse other than to accommodate himself completely.

The problem is that inside he is still the same frightened man. Perceiving that the accommodation is motivated more by fear than by love and the ability to effect a genuine change, the woman in his life often ends up abandoning him anyway.

When Change Is Not Change, But Breakdown

A defeated man reduced to a sycophant: that's how Ian Silver felt for the two years he desperately clung to his relationship with Vera, his wife of ten years. A successful car salesman, Ian spent much of his time on the road while Vera stayed home and raised their only daughter. He thought his marriage was stable—good, in fact. True, Vera often complained that he was overly critical of her housekeeping, but from his vantage point, her housekeeping deserved to be criticized. And yes, he did expect her to tend to him when he was home, and he resented it when dinner was late because she was on the phone talking to one of her girlfriends. But Ian did not view Vera's complaints as a sign of any real trouble. Maybe he wasn't perfect, but neither was she. Besides, there was always money for food on the table and a few luxuries, too. What else could a woman want? When Vera announced that she was taking a job as a management trainee for a local insurance agency, Ian didn't bat an eyelash. She was just a little bored, he told himself. Besides, it would get her off his back.

A year later, Vera told him that she was moving out. She couldn't deal with his condescending attitude, she said. She was tired of being his "slave," an appendage to his success. She had had it with things always being done his way, on his time schedule. Now she wanted a life of her own.

At first, Ian didn't believe her. But when Vera told him she had found an apartment and would be gone in a week, Ian, who had never cried since he had known Vera, became hysterical. "I'll do anything you want," he pleaded, "anything you say. I never knew you were unhappy. Just tell me how you want me to act, and I'll start over again. Another chance, Vera, please. I need you."

Vera heard their daughter crying in her room, and she told Ian she would give their relationship one last chance. But he was going to have to make some dramatic changes. Now that she was working, she wanted him to share the housework. She wanted him to spend more time with both her and their daughter.

Ian agreed, although he knew that Vera's demands were impossible for him to meet. He had always been, as he thought of himself, "a man's man" or, in our words, a Samson. His primary sense of masculinity came from being the dominant one, the one in charge. He was so well-defended that it never dawned on him that his need to control was a symptom of underlying feelings of inferiority. Nor did it occur to him that the road to true adjustment was not passive compliance but expanding himself as a person, understanding that his need to control hurt himself as much as it hurt Vera.

This is an important point. For a man to truly stop being a Samson, he must not only give up his Samson-like ways, but he must also do a lot of soul-searching. He must develop a new identity based on inner security rather than on lording over others. He must understand that to express his vulnerabilities, to develop his emotional, nurturing side, and to relate to a woman as a different but equal individual makes him not only more of a man but a more mature human being.

But Ian was incapable of much soul-searching. He was too rigid and defensive in his ways. In his mind, he had just one out: to give in to Vera's every want and need.

And he did, at least superficially. Almost instantaneously, he became submissive. Whatever Vera wanted to do was fine with him. Wherever Vera wanted to go, he went. Whatever Vera's opinion was, he agreed. True, he was no longer a Samson. Then again, he wasn't much of a person, either. Under the threat of abandonment, he had lost the ability to stand up for himself and had sacrificed his maturity for childlike dependence.

Nine months after Ian's retreat into submission, Vera told him she was leaving for good. She had resented him before, she said, but now she didn't even respect him. She did not want to live with a man that she could step on. A month later, she was out of his life for good.

Ian and Vera's story is typical for the submissive Samson. Unable to adjust and threatened by impending abandonment, he accommodates at the expense of his integrity, his self. He is a sad man to see. But even sadder is the woman who, out of her own feelings of inferiority, remains with him.

What became of Ian? A month after he was left by his wife, he became deeply involved with a younger, dependent woman, and he was able to avert a more overt breakdown. But he also averted a chance to grow.

What happens to the man who is forced to come face-to-face with abandonment by the primary woman in his life? In many cases, a full-fledged overt breakdown is likely to occur.[5] His fears of abandonment and inferiority become real, and they overwhelm him.

On the dark side, a breakdown can totally debilitate a man and scar his relationships with women permanently. The experience may be so painful that he may decide that the risk of getting involved is simply too high. On the bright side, a breakdown can serve as a catalyst to growth, forcing a man to confront his fear and work to overcome it.

In the following story, we'll meet a Samson who used almost every one of the defenses—and when his wife finally left, he had a complete nervous breakdown. It is in many ways the archetypal story of the dilemma of today's Samson: the man who marries and who counts on economic dominance to keep his wife tied to him, only to discover that she now wants more, both from herself and from her marriage. It is also the all-too-common predicament of the woman who rebels, who grows, and who wakes up one day to find that neither the man she married nor the traditional lifestyle she adopted is what she wants.

For as long as June can remember, her *raison d'être* has been to get married and raise a family. She was raised in a traditional Catholic family and aspired to its ideals. Her parents insisted that she go to college as an insurance policy—one could never tell when one might have to support oneself, her father used to say—but her primary goal, her ultimate purpose in life, was to follow the mother-homemaker-wife script that her mother and her mother's mother had followed. She had known nothing else, and therefore she could not conceive of ever wanting anything else.

She met Todd in the spring of 1969, and her family nodded their approval. Two years her senior, Todd, too, was Catholic and believed in a traditional way of life. He was graduating college, was enrolled in officer candidate school, and was going to be commissioned as an officer in the Air Force—in short, he was excellent husband material. And he was head over heels in love with June.

"I saw her as the ideal wife," Todd confided. "She was attractive, bright, loving—the kind of woman who I felt would give me a family and emotional security."

June convinced herself that she was in love with Todd, too, although in retrospect she has her doubts. "He certainly had all the right qualities as a husband, but he was very controlled emotionally, very rigid—the stereotypical military personality. I suppose I told myself that once we got married that would change, he would open up. Besides, my father was very much the same way, so on some level I think I assumed that's just how men were. And I very much wanted to be married."

June and Todd epitomized the coming together of many couples. Both were raised for traditional male-female relationships. Both recognized the script and how the other fit into it.

Neither recognized the danger of following that script blindly or that marriage as primarily an economic exchange ("You love me, and I'll provide for you") is the matrix from which many Samsons are born. There is nothing wrong with the idea of traditional marriage as long as each partner puts his or her love for the other first and emotional and material expectations second. But all too frequently, and often without realizing it, a man counts on his economic power to make up for the love and affection he is not able to express to his wife, and he uses it as an insurance policy against her ever wanting to break out of the traditional female role. Similarly, a woman who is looking for security first and foremost may not consider how well suited a man is for her emotionally when she selects a husband, and she only learns later that she had made a poor choice. Nor does she consider the possibility that she may want to be more than just a homemaker and wife. Now both are in a fix. Over time, the woman starts asking herself, "What am I doing with this man?" or "Is this all there is to life?" The man senses her discontent, and his fear of abandonment is triggered. Economic dominance becomes a necessary tactic to keep the marriage together, and thus is born another Samson.

This is precisely what happened to Todd and June. After their divorce, June admits, "I never even thought about how Todd and I related person to person, whether he was right for me emotionally. And it never occurred to me that his rigidity about traditional sex roles would become a problem, because I never thought I would need anything more than to be a mother and wife to feel fulfilled." Todd, too, understands why the marriage failed. "I always assumed that June would be the emotional backbone of the family, that she would be the woman behind the man. And as long as I had a good job and we were both Catholics, the idea of her ever leaving me never crossed my mind. I can see now that depending on anything other than love and friendship to make a relationship stick does not work."

But at the time, they were naïve. They wanted the same things out of life: a nice, comfortable, middle-class raise-the-kids-mow-the-lawn kind of existence. And they thought that was enough.

They announced their engagement in March, nine months after they met. They married in July and moved to Minnesota, where Todd was stationed. For the next two years, Todd, who was now a lieutenant, pursued his military career; June finished college and obtained her teaching certificate. A week before June was about to begin teaching, she learned she was pregnant.

"I could at least teach half the year, so we'd have some extra money," June suggested.

"Over my dead body," Todd countered. "No pregnant wife of mine is going to work."

June did not protest. "I was thrilled about being pregnant, and the thought of spending nine months decorating the house and setting up the nursery was not totally unappealing. I viewed having a baby as a rite of passage into the kind of life I had always dreamed about."

Tammy, their daughter, was a healthy baby with an equally healthy set of lungs. Todd was thrilled about being a father. But

June found herself inexplicably depressed. She hadn't been prepared for the demands of the baby. She didn't feel any instantaneous sense of fulfillment after its birth. She felt isolated, frightened, and alone. She needed Todd's support desperately.

But Todd was unwilling, or perhaps unable, to respond to June's need. Once he had the responsibility of taking care of a wife and child, he became tunnel-visioned in his devotion to his career in the Air Force. When he returned home from a tiring day, he expected June to cater to him emotionally. "After a long day, I needed June to be there for me, and I didn't have much to give her in return. I didn't really want to be bothered with Tammy; she just seemed like another demand. I guess I felt that since I was bringing in the money, I deserved to be taken care of at home—you know, male prerogative."

That June was working equally hard and that she was having difficulty adjusting to motherhood did not seem to faze him. "Todd wanted me around when he wanted me around. He was very demanding emotionally. But when I'd come to him with a problem about the baby, he'd pretty much tune me out, telling me that it was just postpartum or something." At one point, June suggested hiring a babysitter and getting a job, but Todd exploded. "My wife stays home with her kids where she belongs," he said, adding, "What kind of mother are you anyway?"

Feeling boxed in, with nowhere to go, June tried to push her unhappiness out of her mind. She tried to live with Todd's inability to nourish her emotionally. He was a good, moral man, she told herself, and if he didn't really listen to her, it was because he was preoccupied with providing for their family. He was doing his best. And even her mother agreed that June's place was at home with her young child. What more could she expect? Besides, wasn't this exactly what she had wanted?

The answer was yes, at least in the beginning. She had wanted to live the traditional good life. And Todd fit the bill of providing financial security and upholding the values of the Church completely. But June discovered that there is often an inverse relationship between how dedicated a man is to his career and how emotionally available he is to his wife and family. More to the point, what people think they want does not always turn out to be what they really want.

For the next two years, June lived in a kind of emotional abyss. She denied her loneliness and her resentment of Todd. She denied her disillusionment with motherhood. She denied her boredom. She feigned enthusiasm when she learned that she was once again pregnant.

Then something happened that tore her defenses to shreds. A month after the birth of their second daughter, June's sister was killed in a plane crash. They had been very close, and the loss was devastating for June. She came undone. More than ever, she needed Todd to be there for her emotionally. Instead, Todd was unwilling and unable to hear what she felt about her loss and to console her, and he withdrew.

"He just couldn't deal with it or with my dependence on him," June said. "I felt terribly let down."

So did Todd. Like many men, he had unconsciously turned to June as a mothering figure, someone to be his emotional rock. When that mother broke down, when she came apart, it evoked in him potent feelings of fear. "If Mom is unable to handle her own emotions, how will she take care of me?" says the voice of the dependent little boy, "when I need strength and support?"

Todd was not totally oblivious to June's desperation. "I knew that June needed me. In fact, her sister's death made me decide to get out of the Air Force at the end of my assignment. I could have been very successful staying on, but I realized that I hadn't devoted enough time to my family. So I told my commanding officer that I was going to leave when my enlistment was up."

June remembers feeling touched—and hopeful. "It made me think that maybe I had been wrong about Todd, that maybe under different circumstances he could give me the emotional support that I desperately needed from him."

After his discharge, Todd was offered a job as a manager with a large construction firm in Texas. Both he and June were thrilled to escape the cold Minnesota climate. June hoped it would be the start of a new life, a new phase of their marriage.

However, what was expected to be a move toward more involvement with his family for Todd resulted in even less involvement. What had looked like a golden opportunity turned into a nightmare for him. As bright as he was, he had never held a supervisory position. Even though he had been a military officer, his duties had not included direct supervision. With no experience to fall back on, he was placed in charge of a department of twenty-five people. Of those twenty-five, he was the youngest. "I was fresh off the street. Worse yet," he said, "the man I had beaten out for the job was now working for me."

Todd plunged headfirst into his work. Once again, he was unavailable to June emotionally.

The next six months were the most painful period of June's life. "I had an infant baby, I was mourning the death of my sister, and I felt totally alone, totally vulnerable. I really had to search the depths of my resources to cope. Emotionally speaking, I was completely on my own."

Yet as painful as it was, the experience made her strong. "I had gone through a crisis by myself, and I had come through it. I had found inner strength that I didn't know I'd had."

The experience also made her question her values, what she wanted out of life. "The thought that kept coming up again and again was, 'It could have been me instead of my sister,' and if that were true, how would I want to spend the rest of my life? What did I want for *me*?"

The answers to those questions were disturbing, because very little of the way she was living her life made sense to her. "For the first time, I faced the fact that there was a lot that I wanted from marriage that I was not getting. There was something important missing. And I admitted that I wanted to be more than just a wife and mother."

These questions and their answers at first depressed her; then they frightened her; then they changed her. "After about a year, I emerged as a very different person. I don't know quite how I can put it into words—I was so different that I hardly recognized myself. My whole relationship to the world, to myself, and to Todd had changed."

It would take June a number of years before she had the courage and the resources to actually leave the marriage. She was a Catholic and the mother of two children. From that vantage point alone, divorce seemed almost inconceivable. But even if, after that year, June did not leave Todd physically, emotionally she was, in her own words, "about as far away as I could be."

Todd, too, sensed the difference. But he did not sense that it was not only June's sister's death that had caused the problem but how deeply he had disappointed June by not coming through for her and how unhappy she was with the life she had once thought she wanted.

"There were a few times during that year that June would start yelling at me, saying that I didn't care about her or that she felt the walls closing in on her," Todd remembers. "But it didn't strike me as anything irreparable. I mean, maybe it was true that I was overly involved in my work, but I wanted to get ahead. And I figured that once I started doing better and could afford more, June would feel better. I thought our problems would be over because I believed her talk about going back to work was her way of saying she wanted more material things."

The Breakdown of Economic Dominance

A year and a half after the death of June's sister, Todd's boss called him into his office. "Look, I don't know how to tell you this, but I really don't think you can handle the job you're in. I know you need the money, so what I've decided to do is give you a chance at the foreman's job."

Todd's ego was badly shaken. But he had a family to support. He tried to swallow his pride, but to no avail. Six months later he was fired after he got into a fight with one of the other foremen.

For the next four months, Todd desperately sought work. The bills mounted. "Well, it looks like *I'm* going to have to go out and get a job," June finally said one night over dinner.

"It was so humiliating," Todd recalls. "She didn't say it outright, but I had this feeling that she didn't think much of me as a man."

"It's true," June admitted, "but not in the way Todd thought. Until then, he was at least taking care of me financially. But now he wasn't even doing that. It made me I realize that aside from money, there really was very little else he had given me."

June and Todd's situation honed in on the realities of many withdrawing and economically dominant Samsons' fear: "Other than money, what am I good for?"

June found work within two weeks. The local grade school was short on substitute teachers, and June worked almost every day. Her mood went from lethargic to energetic. "I think that deep down I believed that I couldn't take care of myself financially, that I was really dependent on Todd to do that for me. But now that I was out in the world, even though my salary was small, I had a new sense about myself, a feeling that 'I can even do this without him!'"

While June was enjoying a feeling of newfound confidence, Todd was feeling that he was losing control. He felt June's growing distance. His economic dominance had crumbled, and the other defenses quickly came into play.

Withdrawal and Possessiveness

Todd had been withdrawn before, but now he pulled away from June and his family almost completely. "He was so consumed with job hunting that he became a total stranger."

At the same time, Todd became extremely possessive. He didn't want June to continue with the PTA. He made a scene every time she went to her bowling league. He didn't want her to go out with her friends.

"He became very suspicious," June told us, "and that seemed strange to me because he had never minded before. But now, every time I went out, he'd ask me, 'Where are you going? Who are you going with? What are you doing?' And every time I went out, there'd be a blowout when I came home."

The hostility, Todd's increasing need to control her, made June's resentment more acute. More and more, she felt the need to get away from him. "I reached the point where I just didn't give a damn if he objected or gave me a hard time. My friends were my only escape."

Todd was outraged. It was the first time June had outwardly defied him. But there was something else, too. "I realized for the first time how much of her life had nothing to do with me, how she had built a life of her own without my even knowing it. Her independence threatened me. The thing that frightened me the most was not being unemployed, but the possibility that the marriage would break up. And it wouldn't be me walking out on her."

That realization made Todd panic, and his panic threw him into the third line of defense. He became increasingly violent, going into fits of rage. He threw things. He started pushing June around, insulting her in front of the children. But Todd's attempts to control June, wrought out of his fear of losing her, only pushed her farther away.

"I grew to really resent him. I resented his suspicion. I resented that he was trying to control my life. I resented his rigidity about women's roles." In essence, June resented Todd's strong and ever-increasing fear.

Todd was no longer blind to June's feelings. "By that time, I knew the marriage was really shaky." Yet despite his perception, Todd clung to the notion that things would be fine if only he could find a job, if only he could put his first line of defense back in place.

After months of looking, Todd finally was offered a position as a state employee. The problem was that it was in another part of Texas, and June refused to move. Todd felt he had no choice but to go, and for the next eight months he commuted home on weekends.

During this period, June began to take direct action to free herself from her marriage. She decided to go for her master's degree in special education. At first, Todd scoffed, then he became hostile, but her mind was made up. She was going to take control of her life financially, whether Todd liked it or not.

There was still the problem of religion. By this time, June knew that she had to find a way out, but her religious background told her that divorce was wrong. One of her close friends in graduate school, an ex-nun, suggested she seek counseling from a liberal priest in the area. She did, and when she told Todd she was in therapy, he seemed to approve. "I just assumed that he would tell her that she would have to find a way to make the marriage work," Todd told us, "and that relieved me."

Shortly thereafter, Todd received a job transfer back home, and that relieved him, too. "I thought I had it made. I had a stable job with the government. I still had my paycheck from the reserve. I was making a decent living, and I could support my family again. Everything seemed to be falling back into place, and I was sure my marriage would follow."

Todd was so convinced that his failure as a financial provider was the only source of his marital problems that when he came home and June told him she was moving to the bedroom down the hall, he couldn't understand it. "I was solid in my work at the time, so I just denied what was happening. I told myself that June just needed some space, some time to recuperate from the years of problems we'd had." His voice choked up. "Now I know that there was not enough space that I could have given her."

Even more certain was his conviction that his religion would protect him against the possibility of divorce.

One day, June called Todd at the office. "Come home early tonight," she told him. "It's urgent."

"What's wrong?" he asked June, who was sitting on the bed when he got home.

"I'm filing for divorce," she told him.

June remembers Todd's reaction as if it were yesterday. "He just glared at me, and then, without raising his voice a decibel, he said, 'That's impossible. You're a Catholic. The Church won't let you.'"

June repeated her intention.

"You'll never get a divorce from me," he said, storming into the bathroom. A few minutes later he emerged, apparently composed. "I'm going out for a walk," he announced. Then, halfway out the door, he said, "By the way, when did you get too good to clean the toilet bowl?"

Todd returned a few hours later, the smell of bourbon hanging on his breath. "I want to see that therapist priest you've been seeing," he said.

The following Tuesday, Todd walked into the priest's office with the zeal of one who is certain that he is about to meet his strongest ally.

"June has told me that she is filing for divorce," Todd began. "And of course, I have already told her that as a Catholic she cannot do that."

The priest shook his head sadly. "Listen, Todd, I understand how badly you feel, but you might as well forget it. Your marriage is over."

Todd became incensed. "What do you mean? You're a priest!"

"That's true, and when June first came for counseling, I suggested that she try to make the marriage work. I believe in the sanctity of marriage as much as you do. But over time, it became clear that I was not going to change her mind, even if I threatened to excommunicate her from the Church."

Todd became agitated. "Look, I know we've gone through a rough financial period, but now I'm working again. I'm sure if she gave it a chance, the marriage could be repaired."

"If losing your job were the issue, it probably could be. But the problem, Todd, is that June has been emotionally distant from you for years, long before you lost your job. She feels that you have let her down emotionally, that you haven't been sensitive to her needs as a person, and that is not so easily fixed."

Todd was stunned. He had never realized, had been too busy to realize, that the roots of his marital discord went a lot deeper than his financial problems. "Look, I can try harder, be better. . . ." The priest let Todd vent his feelings until he had nothing more to say.

"I'm sorry," the priest said sympathetically. "If you need to talk this out some more, feel free to call me."

When Todd returned home, June told him that she had found an apartment for herself and the children. She moved out the following night. When he found himself alone in his house, the abandonment finally began to sink in. All he could think was, "One way or another, I am going to stop her from doing this. I am going to make her come back."

His worst fear a reality, Todd began to fall apart completely.

Sabotage and Breakdown

Three weeks after June left, Todd sneaked into her garage and stole June's car, leaving her with no way to get to work. On another occasion, he went away with the children for the weekend and told June that if she went through with the divorce, he would move away and never let her see them.

"I was flabbergasted," June recounted. "Somehow I always believed that despite everything, Todd was a rational person. I guess," she said reflectively, "by that point, he was really half out of his mind. He really believed that by threatening me, he would get me to go back to him."

The worst was yet to come.

His experience with the priest and the knowledge that June's closest friends were ex-nuns made him paranoid. There was nothing he could count on anymore—not even the Church, which he had always regarded as the most stable force in his life. He became convinced that anyone who had known June since they had moved had been trying to get June to leave him, that she would have stayed had it not been for their influence. His desperation climaxed when Todd wrote to the bishop of his home state, telling him that there was a conspiracy against him, that everyone that June knew who was involved with the Church had been trying to coax her into a divorce.

To this day, June seethes when she tells the story. "The bishop responded by investigating my therapist and any friend that I had who had anything to do with my Church. That was really the end for me. Since that point, I have not had a good feeling toward Todd."

Even now, Todd sees it differently. "Were June not under the influence of those people, I think our marriage would have repaired itself." He does not see that religion was yet another failed defense against his ultimate fear.

The bishop's investigation showed no wrongdoing on the part of June, her friends, or the priest. Todd now felt abandoned not only by his wife but by his religion. All three lines of defense had failed. He was a man alone with his fear.

The anxiety was unbearable, and Todd began drinking heavily. But the alcohol did not anesthesize him; rather, it made him violent and irrational. Night after night, Todd would drink himself into a stupor and call June up, begging for her to take him back. When June responded with silence, he became obscene. Things became so bad, June said, that she considered changing her telephone number, but she decided against it because she feared such a move would only incite Todd even more.

Their nightly phone ritual stopped when, four months after their separation, Todd called June's house and heard an unfamiliar voice at the other end.

"Who the hell is this?" Todd said menacingly.

"I'm Betty, the babysitter."

"Where is my wife?" he commanded.

"I'm sorry, sir, but she said not to give out any information over the phone."

"She's gone out with a man, right, *right*?" he screamed, slamming down the phone.

Betty was frightened, and she called June at the number she had left. June's date brought her home immediately and walked her to the door. "Will you be all right?" he asked with genuine concern.

"She'll be fine," snarled Todd, who had been sitting at the side of the house waiting for June to come home for the past hour. Then, seeming to have lost all control, Todd grabbed June's date and threw him to the ground. "If you ever so much as come near my wife again, I'll kill you," he said.

June ran into the house and called the police, but by the time they arrived, Todd was nowhere to be seen. A few hours later, they found him at the old train yard, bleeding and unconscious. Todd had driven his car into a parked train. His head had gone full force through the windshield. Had he been found an hour later, he would have been dead.

The doctors told June that Todd was fortunate. He had suffered a severe concussion and lost a lot of blood, but given his injuries, he shouldn't have even still been alive. That isn't to say that Todd was left unscathed. When he left the hospital two weeks later, he had a five-inch scar running from his left temple to his jawbone that doctors say will remain visible for the rest of his life.

The real scar, one might guess, is not on his face but in his heart. "I know that Todd desperately wanted me to feel sorry for him, to take care of him after his accident," June said sadly. "But I couldn't. I felt it was just another way of trying to get me to go back to him. The way it felt was, 'I'm going to keep you with me even if I have to incapacitate myself.' I think he wanted me to feel pity, but all I felt was that Todd was pathetic."

We do not know Todd's side of it. In our interview with him, he never once mentioned the incident with the train. Nor did he appear self-conscious about his scar. It is a part of his life, one suspects, that he would rather not think about, that he prefers to forget.

The Road to Recovery

It has been three years since June and Todd's divorce was finalized, years during which Todd has painstakingly reconstructed his life.

"There have been a number of areas in my life that have taken off like a rocket," Todd told us. "I have had major success on the job. I have had major success in the Air Force; I was promoted twice in two years. I have done volunteer work for the Texas Republican party, and I feel that I am tremendously respected by people."

More important, Todd told us, is that he understands himself better. "I realize that I have a need to be close to, dependent on a woman. Also, from speaking to women at work who are divorced, I've begun to see that it isn't enough to be a financial provider in a marriage; most women want a man who shows he cares, who is there in an emotional way. For a long time I was convinced that my being out of work had created a pattern of disrespect that was the source of the breakup. In some way, I still think that's true. But I have to admit that, looking back, there were major emotional ways that June needed me and that I let her down."

Over the years, Todd began to understand that his emotional withdrawal was detrimental to himself as well. "I don't know exactly what made me realize that I had been duped by the traditional male role. Maybe it was when I realized that if I lost June, I might also lose the kids, too. But something started to really change in here." He pointed to his stomach. "It was as if I began seeing that I was missing out on the whole emotional side of life, that I was nothing but a work machine. I had fantasies of being on my deathbed and having all the things I'd done in my life, all the 'accomplishments,' flash in front of my eyes. And the way it felt was, 'Big deal. What about love? What about feelings?' It shook me up, and I think I've begun to relate to people in a more open, caring way."

June, too, has seen the growth in Todd.

"He realizes that he really wasn't emotionally very giving," June said, "and he's grown. And his attitude toward women has changed quite a bit, really. He's still traditional and rigid in a lot of ways, but he's also opened up his eyes. I've met a few of the women that he works with, and they say he's very supportive, not at all chauvinistic. They say he's one of the few men in the office that treats women as equals. That's helped not only in terms of me but in terms of our girls. In the past couple of years, he's been very supportive of their desires to have careers. He's also made friends with a married woman who is a feminist, and although he tells me he doesn't always agree with her, he has listened to her. I think that's because she's been married for a long time and is very devoted to her husband and kids as well as to her career. It's as if she's saying, 'Not all women who want to be independent are bitches; they don't all do men in.' I don't know what's behind all these changes, but it's been for the better."

Their relationship, both told us, is also better. "I think that June and I have a very good agreement," Todd said. "We always make the kids a priority, and we are both flexible in terms of who has the kids when. I've come through for June in terms of taking care of the kids even when it wasn't my day to do so, and she's done the same for me. Actually, I think that June has a much better deal with me for an ex-husband than most women get."

He is right about that. Many men, after being abandoned by their wives, engage in malicious games of sabotage and are completely uncooperative to the point of allowing their rage to interfere with their wives' relationships with their children.

Yet speaking to June, one gets the sense that there is something behind Todd's willingness to help more than a desire to keep the communication lines open. "It's true that Todd is very cooperative," she admitted. "But every once in a while I feel that he goes out of his way because deep down, he still feels that I will someday go back to him. I don't think he's really integrated the fact that I would never, never consider going back to him." It was for this reason, June said, that she almost did not grant us an interview. "When I heard what your book was about, I knew I had an important story to tell. At the same time, I didn't want to say anything that would in the least way give Todd the impression that I wanted to go back with him. Please say that if you use my story. Tell him that I wish he would go on with his life."

Is there any credence to June's perception?

Sadly, there is. "There are times when I'd like to tell myself that the reason June hasn't gotten seriously involved with anyone else is that she thinks our marriage is reparable, too," Todd confessed. "But deep down, I know that's a dream that I need to hold on to, at least for a little while longer. I'm working on it, but I know I'm not quite there."

In making such an admission, both to us and to himself, however, Todd is halfway home.

PART II

WORKING TOWARD CHANGE

A Word About Change

By now, it should be clear that a Samson's hidden fear of women, as well as his need to control them, which is a result of that fear, creates tremendous difficulties for both sexes. Even when the controls Samsons enforce do not push the women they love out of their lives, they lose out because there is no way to be happy in a relationship when you're running scared all the time. Women lose out because there is no way to feel good about a partner whose idea of a partnership is "Do as I say." In the long run, the whole of society suffers because, until women and men can have reciprocal, free-of-fear relationships, their children will continue to grow up believing that men and women are not friends but enemies.

So what can be done? More specifically, as a woman, what can you do?

As paradoxical as it might seem, the place to start is by accepting what you *cannot* do. All too often, women who are involved with a Samson express extreme frustration. "I've done everything in my power to force him to change, but nothing works" is a commonly heard complaint. "How does a molehill move a mountain?" The answer, of course, is that it doesn't. You do not have the power to make anyone else change. No person has the power to change anyone but himself or herself.

This is an important point. The faster you give up the

idea that you will be able to rescue a Samson from his plight or convince him to see things from your point of view by nagging, threatening, or even well-intentioned arm-twisting, the better off you will be. While you might be motivated by good intentions, these coercive tactics are rarely effective. In fact, they often yield the opposite result.

But if you can't force a man to change, then what *can* you do? Should you resign yourself to living with men's fears? Not at all. Although you cannot change a man, you can be instrumental in creating a climate that will help motivate him to change because he comes to the conclusion on his own that change is in his best interest.

The first step toward establishing such an environment is understanding the ways in which you might be contributing to a man's fears. In Chapter 9, you will learn whether you do contribute to men's fears and, if you do, what you can do to get rid of your Delilah-like traits. You cannot provide an atmosphere free of fear if you are giving a man good reason to fear you.

In Chapter 10, we discuss some general ideas about change. If your expectations about change are unreasonable, there is no way that you can come out ahead. We call this chapter the TLC's of change, because change takes *time*, you will have to take the *lead*, and you can expect *conflict*.

Chapter 11 is designed for the woman who wants to help her Samson overcome his fear. It offers a step-by-step approach to confronting a Samson. Chapter 12 offers suggestions on how to deal with the crisis that is likely to result when you do.

Chapter 13 is specifically for men. Chances are, if a man is a tried-and-true Samson, he will not read it on his own. But for those men who are more flexible, this chapter can set them on the right track to overcoming their fear once and for all. If your Samson resists reading the chapter, we strongly suggest you urge him to read it because it could truly help improve your relationship.

Chapter 9

Recognizing the Delilah in Yourself – A Test to Help You

When Bill Jenks, thirty-eight, married his wife, Tess, ten years ago, he wanted to believe that she was every bit as much in love with him as he was with her. He knew that one of the reasons Tess was attracted to him was that he was an entrepreneur who looked as if he were going places. What he did not know was that his potential as a money-maker was not just one of several reasons she married him, but the only one.

The truth about Tess emerged in small, telltale pieces. Their sex life, for example, had a certain rhythm: when Bill was doing well, Tess was turned on; when business was floundering, Tess lost interest. She didn't seem to care about the stress that Bill was under to give her the material things she wanted. At one career low point, Bill was on the verge of collapsing from exhaustion, but Tess kept pushing for the bigger house, the better car, the designer clothes.

The real proof of Tess's feelings came after Bill decided to go into another line of business. True, it would mean struggling for a while, but Bill was tired of what he was doing, and he desperately needed a change. Tess was adamantly against the move. "You're looking for trouble," she admonished. Bill ignored her. A month later, he came home to find his house emptied of all its contents.

His bank account had also been cleaned out. Tess did not leave so much as a note announcing her departure. Bill later learned that Tess had been having an affair with a man who was independently wealthy, a man whom, after their divorce, she married.

"Women are users who can't be trusted as far as you can throw them," Bill told us, summarizing his feelings.

Bob Samuels, forty-one, truly wanted to find an independent-minded woman, and when he met Suzanne, he was convinced he had found her. A stockbroker who earned $40,000 a year, Suzanne seemed committed to the ideology of equal rights. She strongly believed that men and women should share the financial burden of supporting a family as well as the day-to-day chores of running the household and caring for children. Bob couldn't have agreed more.

After the arrival of their first child, however, Suzanne abandoned her egalitarian point of view. "I have decided that I'd rather not work anymore," she announced one evening. "After all, babies are only babies for a short while," she said, ending all discussion of the subject. Bob was incensed. "I thought we had an agreement to share both the financial obligations and the childrearing functions. Besides, how are we going to live on my income alone?" Suzanne's answer was blunt enough. "Well, we'll have to cut back, or you'll have to get a better job. I've made up my mind."

Bob did find a new job for more money, but he detested it. When, after two years of full-time motherhood, Suzanne told Bob she wanted to return to work, he was elated. "Now that you'll be working again, I think I'd like to take some time off from this treadmill I'm on and figure out what I'd really like to do professionally," he told her.

The suggestion raised Suzanne's hackles. "You can't be serious," she said. "One of the main reasons I want to go back to work is because I'm tired of feeling that we're living hand to mouth."

"I thought you wanted an egalitarian relationship," Bob countered.

"I do," Suzanne responded, seemingly oblivious to the contradiction implicit in her attitude. "But I never agreed to be the sole breadwinner of the family!"

Bob did not want to break up his family, so he agreed to "compromise": Suzanne went back to work, and Bob took a new job that paid slightly less but that he enjoyed slightly more. But to this day, the disillusionment remains. "She believes in liberation, all right," Bob said with an edge of resentment, *"her* liberation."

Nick Olsen, twenty-nine, says that he has been turned off by many women because they seem to harbor a lot of animosity toward men. "The attitude that comes across is that all men are no damn good. I see it everywhere. Sometimes at lunch, I'll overhear two women talking about what idiots their husbands are. I've also met a lot of women who get really riled up if you so much as open a door for them. The worst kind, though, are those women who seem to enjoy intimidating a man. Then there are these women managers who are more ruthless than the worst men. As far as I can see, the only thing that the women's movement has done is to turn women against men, and then they are flabbergasted when men respond negatively to them."

What do all these men have in common? Each fears women because women have given him a good reason to be fearful. Each has come face to face with a Delilah.

It is hard to live with fear, as we have seen in the preceding chapters. The pain and stress that men suffer as a result can be excruciating. What is even more painful, however, is that most men experience more fear than is warranted by reality. The vast majority of women want to have intimate relationships with men. Indeed, if there is any aspect of women's upbringing that is superior to men's, it is their desire to attach, to empathize, to use their strength for cooperative purposes. The feminine way of looking out for oneself is to consider the needs of others as well as those of oneself.[1] Even when women are in positions of power, they tend to opt for a cooperative rather than a competitive strategy.[2] The goal of women has never been to lord it over men or to psychologically castrate them. They simply want to be treated as men's equals. Whether they work in or outside the home, women want their contribution to the family and to society to be considered as significant as that of men. They do not desire to control their relationships with men, but they crave a sense of partnership that flourishes on mutual love and respect. Nor do most women want to be "female" men. They, however, want to be loved for being both female and independent.

At the same time, there is some truth to men's fear of women, because some women do act like Delilah—exploiting, confusing, belittling men. These women exploit men's weaknesses, their vulnerability, using them as weapons against them. Unless a woman overcomes the Delilah in her, she cannot possibly hope to help her Samson overcome his fear.

Are you a Delilah? The test on the following pages will help you decide. When taking the test, try to be as honest as you can about yourself. This will not be easy, because it is difficult to acknowledge aspects of ourselves that are not particularly nice. But honesty is essential if you really want to help.

THE DELILAH TEST

The test below is divided into three parts, one for each type of Delilah.

Using the following scale as a guide, circle the number below the response that best describes your feelings or attitude. Add up the numbers you have circled and record your score on the subtotal line at the end of each part.

I am like this:

Never or Rarely	*Occasionally*	*Often*	*Very Often*
0	1	2	3

Part I: The Beguiling Delilah

Your respect for a man largely depends on how much money, prestige, or power he has.

0	1	2	3

You would consider marrying a wealthy man even if you were not in love with him.

0	1	2	3

When the man in your life does well professionally, you feel good about yourself; when he does poorly, you feel bad about yourself.

0	1	2	3

Deep down, you expect a man to rescue you from having to take care of yourself financially.

0	1	2	3

You have dated a man you didn't like because he had enough money to take you to fine places.

0	1	2	3

If your mate said that he was unhappy at his job and wanted to take another job he liked better for less money, you would feel angry, resentful, or betrayed.

0   1   2   3

BEGUILING DELILAH SUBTOTAL _____

PART II: THE CONFLICTED DELILAH

You enjoy being taken care of by a man, but you resent it at the same time.

0   1   2   3

You want a man to be emotionally sensitive, but if he is too emotional, you think of him as a wimp.

0   1   2   3

You want to be independent, but you feel that a man is standing in your way.

0   1   2   3

You want to make your own decisions, but you find yourself looking to the man in your life to make them for you.

0   1   2   3

You feel that a man should take care of you because you have been held back by a male-dominated society.

0   1   2   3

You feel that women should have the choice of working or not working, but that men should not have the same choice.

0   1   2   3

CONFLICTED DELILAH SUBTOTAL: _____

Part III: The Contemptuous Delilah

Other than for sex or money, you feel that you don't need men.

     0   1   2   3

You think that men are basically selfish, egotistical, or neurotic.

     0   1   2   3

You think that men's hobbies, such as watching sports or playing poker, are silly male habits.

     0   1   2   3

You think of men as the enemy.

     0   1   2   3

You have an urge to get back at men.

     0   1   2   3

You talk with your friends about what idiots men are.

     0   1   2   3

CONTEMPTUOUS DELILAH SUBTOTAL: _____

Now that you have completed the test, turn the page and learn how to interpret your scores.

Interpreting Your Delilah Test Score

Use the following guide to help you pinpoint the degree to which you possess Delilah-like traits. First, place your score for each section of the test in the space provided below:

The Delilah Test Results
The Score

Part I: The Beguiling Delilah   _____
Part II: The Conflicted Delilah   _____
Part III: The Contemptuous Delilah   _____

Now that you have placed your scores in one place for easy reference, read the general interpretation of the scores that follows.

If your score is less than 6 on any part of the test: From time to time, you might think or act like a Delilah, but basically your motivation to betray or hurt men is minimal.

If your score is between 6 and 12 on any part of the test: Delilah is definitely more than a minuscule part of your personality, and there is a good chance that that message is coming across loud and clear to the man or men in your life. It is also likely that you feel frustrated in your relationships with men, but until now, you have not acknowledged your own role in creating that frustration.

If your score is 13 or more on any part of the test: A large part of you functions as a Delilah, and you are a real threat to men. Chances are, you have some deep, unresolved problems about yourself as a woman and your relationships with men. You may gain some insight into the causes of your feelings and behaviors by reading the resolution part of this chapter, but you should seek professional help if you ever want to have positive relationships with men.

What Kind of Delilah Are You?

Now take another look at your responses in each of the test's three sections. Do any of your scores for any of the separate parts add up to more than 6? If so, chances are that you lean toward being a certain kind of Delilah.

Below, we will briefly summarize the three primary types of Delilahs and the influences that act as catalysts in their development.

The Beguiling Delilah

If your highest score in the three sections of the Delilah Test is for Part I, you lean toward being a Beguiling Delilah. The Beguiling Delilah is the "classic" Delilah in the sense that she, like her biblical counterpart, knows how to get what she wants from a man by preying on his sexual and emotional weaknesses. What she most often wants is to be taken care of financially, as did Bill Jenks's wife, Tess.

How many women are there who, like Delilah, use their feminine charms to get men "into the palm of their hands" or to "wrap men around their little pinkies"? To one degree or another, probably all women do. Many women are trained from an early age in the arts of feminine allure—coquettishness, helplessness, seductiveness—and they use these as a way of attracting men. Of course, flirting to attract a man's attention does not make a Delilah. On the contrary, men often enjoy these male-female games as much as women do, and they rarely view them as manipulations or betrayals, because there is no deception involved. The man is every bit as aware of what is going on as the woman.

The Beguiling Delilah is different because she deceives a man to extract what she wants from him; she uses his vulnerabilities to get him to do her bidding. She leads him into believing that she really cares for him as a person, when deep down she is looking out only for her needs. Her intent is not necessarily to hurt him; his feelings simply are not her primary concern. To her, he is a provider first and a person second.

The Conflicted Delilah

If your highest score is in Part II of the test, you are a Conflicted Delilah. In terms of men, you are perhaps the most feared of all because your spoken message is "Give up those old Samson ways of yours," while the unspoken message is "Only give up those Samson ways that make my life difficult, but keep the rest." Either way, a man bearing the brunt of these messages is in trouble. If he continues to be the Samson he is, you resent him, perhaps to the point of eventually leaving him. If he gives up his control and becomes the egalitarian, sensitive man you want him to be, you also resent him, and you may think about ending your relationship with him.

The Conflicted Delilah comes in two main varieties. The most common is the "Have your cake and eat it, too" vintage, represented by Bob Samuels's wife, Suzanne. On the surface, a woman like this appears to believe in equality between the sexes, yet when it boils down to action, what she really means is that women should have a choice about what they do with their lives, but men should not. Unfortunately, the man who is attracted to this type of Delilah takes her egalitarian veneer at face value, only to learn later that he has been taken for a ride.

The second type of Conflicted Delilah is the one who is confused about her feelings about independence. She very much wants to be independent and make her own way, yet she is insecure about her ability to do so. Often, this conflict leads her into the arms of an economically dominant Samson, but she is ambivalent about him, too. She needs him to be the dominant one in the relationship on one level, but she detests that need at the same time. Unaware of her own conflict, she takes her anger and frustration out on him.

If, during the course of her relationship, she does begin to develop her own autonomy, she steps up her attack against the man in her life. The same dominance that she once needed now arouses the full force of her wrath. She becomes overtly hostile toward her mate, and unless he does a complete about-face, she often leaves him without warning or sympathy. She tells herself that she is running away from his dominance. In truth, she is running away from her old self, her old dependence.

Occasionally, a Conflicted Delilah of this type marries a non-Samson. She is a fortunate woman, indeed. Her partner does not feed into her dependence. On the contrary, he is often instrumental in helping her overcome it. With his support, she may become truly independent in time. When this is the case, she appreciates her spouse for life.

The Contemptuous Delilah

If your highest score is in Part III of the Delilah Test, you have the characteristics of the Contemptuous Delilah. Although she very well may be involved in relationships with men, deep down she harbors an intense anger, even hatred toward them. She is the type of woman that Nick Olsen addresses, the woman whose underlying message toward men is that they are no damn good.

Their contempt comes out in a number of ways. Some women, particularly if they are economically dependent, may not disparage a man to his face, but they get a real charge out of belittling him behind his back. Others demean men by going out of their way to prove how little they need them or by stating outright that they think men are worthless. Then there are women like those Nick mentioned at the beginning of this chapter: bitterly angry women who publicly state their contempt for men for all the world to hear. Germaine Greer, for example, was quoted in *People* magazine as saying, "I sleep with men. I don't expect anything else from them."[3]

Whether from a homemaker or an angry woman, the sentiment is the same: the male sex is inferior and deserves to be demeaned. As Samson described himself after his hair was cut off, today's man is, to a growing number of women, "nothing but an object of derision." It is a message that strikes at the core of men's deepest fear: not only that women may be superior but that they will use that superiority to demean men and to try to lord over them.

Getting Past Delilah: It's Up to You

Whether Beguiling, Conflicted, or Contemptuous, all the Delilahs have one thing in common: all contribute to men's fear by giving men good reason to fear them. Thus, it is virtually impossible for a woman to help a Samson overcome his fear if she has strong Delilah characteristics.

If you see any of these Delilahs in yourself, you have a decision to make. You have to get rid of your Delilah characteristics, live without a man, or learn to live with a man who is a Samson.

You might be wondering why a woman would choose *not* to stop being a Delilah. Sadly, there is a very good reason. Just as there are some outward benefits of being a Samson, for example, economic power, there are some built-in payoffs to being a Delilah. The Beguiling Delilah may not have an emotionally intimate relationship with a man, but to the extent that she is successful in baiting a man with her feminine allure, she usually doesn't have to worry about her day-to-day financial existence. Perhaps the Conflicted Delilah isn't quite at peace with herself, but she often does get to have the advantages of liberation without the responsibilities that go hand in hand with independence. The anger of the Contemptuous Delilah may prevent her from feeling good about the man in her life or about men in general, but she receives vindictive pleasure from turning the tables and making men feel inferior.

If you are determined to work through your type of Delilah, you must be willing to forgo these payoffs. A good place to begin is to analyze whether you have a subconscious commitment to keeping a man at least a partial Samson. Do you, for example, complain that the Samson in your life withdraws into his work, but at the same time enjoy the material benefits that his workaholism provides? Do you despise the fact that he puts you down for acting like a "princess" while at the same time feeling that you deserve to be catered to? Do you harbor feelings of contempt toward a man but remain unwilling to consider the possibility of leaving him? Do you secretly want him to continue being a Samson in some ways but not in others, thereby placing him in an impossible double bind?

These questions are difficult to ask and even harder to answer because they force you to confront some unpleasant truths about yourself and your contribution to men's fears. Yet that is precisely where you must begin. It takes courage to face the Delilah that lurks within you, and even more courage to do something about getting rid of her. It takes time to overcome completely the psychological underpinnings that give rise to the Delilah in you, but there is one thing that you can do immediately.

Eliminate Delilah-like Behavior

You can stop being a contributor to men's fears by immediately eliminating as many Delilah-like behaviors from your repertoire as possible. You can do this even before you have a clear understanding of what motivates you to be a Delilah in the first place. Behavior *can* be modified without full insight into, or resolution of, our deep, internal conflicts. Changing one's behavior can often lead to a change in one's more deeply rooted attitudes as effectively as can resolving one's internal conflicts first and then altering one's behavior. Given the complexity of human motivation, the behavioral approach to change is usually a lot faster.

If you are a single Beguiler, turn down dates with men in whom your primary interest is being wined and dined lavishly. As a married Beguiler, you need to look at your spouse as a person with feelings and needs and start attending to those needs. If you are a Conflicted Delilah, stop putting the man in your life in "damned if you do, damned if you don't" situations. Take the blame off your man's shoulders by admitting that you have dumped your own conflicts on him. The remedy of the Contemptuous Delilah is simple: stop, think, and stay silent every time you are about to make one of your "all men are no good" statements; and don't indulge your impulse to belittle or patronize men.

It may sound unrealistic to assume that you can eradicate your Delilah behaviors immediately, but you really can. If you are genuinely committed to helping men overcome their fears, you will be alert to all the things you do and say that stir those fears. If you find yourself acting like a Delilah, acknowledge that your behavior is your problem and apologize for it as soon as possible. You should encourage your husband, lover, or friend to point out any Delilah-like behavior as soon as he sees it.

It is not uncommon for a man to stop acting like a Samson once his mate stops acting like a Delilah. This is particularly true when a woman has had an unconscious commitment to keeping her man a Samson, when she has positively reinforced his Samson-like ways. In other cases, however, a man will not automatically stop being a Samson when a woman stops acting like a Delilah because some men are full-fledged Samsons even before they meet a Delilah. Why, then, should you go through all this work to give up the Delilah in you?

Giving up your Delilah may not be, in and of itself, a miracle cure for turning a Samson into a non-Samson, but erasing the ways you contribute to a man's fear almost always results in some reduction in his Samson-like behavior. More important, as long as you are a Delilah, the prescriptions for helping a Samson overcome his fear that are presented in the following chapters will be ineffective. You cannot expect a man to stop being afraid as long as you are giving him just cause for his fear.

Delving Deeper

At the same time as you are working on no longer acting like a Delilah, you must understand the reason you are a Delilah in the first place. This step is a lot more difficult than just altering your behavior because the roots of a Delilah are often as deep as those of a Samson. On the following pages, we will summarize the dynamics that create the various Delilahs and discuss some remedies you can begin to use to work through those dynamics. These remedies take time, however, and in some cases, a Delilah may need professional counseling to truly break free of her past. This does not mean that you cannot begin acting on some of the suggestions for helping men overcome their fears that we offer in the following chapters. As long as you have ceased acting like a Delilah and are committed to working through the conflicts that create her, you will be in a position to assist men in overcoming their fears.

Keeping this in mind, let's look at how each of the Delilahs gets to be that way.

For the Beguiling Delilah: A Matter of Self-Esteem

If you are a Beguiling Delilah who has successfully lured men with your charms, you may appear to be quite powerful. Certainly, most men will perceive you that way. But behind the manipulative facade of the Beguiling Delilah, there is almost always a woman who experiences herself, on an unconscious level at least, as anything *but* powerful. In fact, the reason that a Beguiling Delilah needs to resort to using her feminine wiles to attract a man is that attaching herself to a more successful "other" is the only way she knows how to feel good about herself.

At heart, a Beguiling Delilah is a woman with very little self-esteem. She feels that she has no potential to make much of herself in the world. The message that she is "only" a woman, that she doesn't have what it takes to make it on her own, frequently begins early at home. Mom, if not incompetent, clearly is less powerful than Dad. Mom may be the woman behind the man, but she's not the person next to him, his equal.

What the Beguiling Delilah learns at home is repeatedly reinforced by the outside world: it is not women who have power, but men. The Margaret Thatchers of the world are exceptions to the rule, few and far between. The women who have the most power are women who are attached to powerful men: Jacqueline Kennedy, Nancy Reagan, Princess Diana. Looking around her, a woman begins to integrate the idea that women are inferior to men, that the only way she will ever become someone, the only way that she can be worthwhile, is to attach herself to someone who is important and worthwhile. To the Beguiling Delilah, catching the right man is a desperate attempt to compensate for her own sense of powerlessness, her own lack of self-esteem.

In their book *Cinderella and Her Sisters*, Ann and Barry Ulanov describe Beguiling Delilahs' feelings about men perfectly: "He is a self-object, chosen to enhance themselves; he is not a real other in his own right. . . . Feeling so empty of goodness in themselves, they lunge violently at the men outside them . . . trying to fill up that emptiness." A woman like this, say the authors, grabs onto a male as a substitute for her own unfulfilled sense of self. "She wants what he has, or what she thinks he has: his power, his position, his sexual organ and whatever it may represent. She reduces him to a part-object . . . and fails to see him as a man, or herself as a woman, either of them as a whole person in his or her own right."[4] Of course, a woman must first catch a man before she can look to him to make up for what she herself does not possess. She does this by using her feminine allure, which she has learned early in life is her best—and often her only—weapon.

Sometimes a Beguiling Delilah's motives are so deep that she may not even be aware of them herself. "It was only after my husband lost his job that I recognized that I had never really loved him, that I had been mostly in love with the fact that he was a good provider." These are the words of a woman who left her husband after he decided to give up a lucrative practice as a podiatrist to become a social worker. "I'm not saying that I knew that when I married him," she added. "I mean, you're supposed to marry for love, right? Looking back, I suppose that I convinced myself that I really did love him. It was only when he wasn't the good provider anymore that my true feelings came out. The sad thing is that if he had not changed professions, I might never have known that I was deluding myself." Moreover, she may never have been forced to come to grips with her own underlying feelings of inadequacy.

Indeed, the first step toward ridding yourself of your Beguiling Delilah is to acknowledge your relatively low opinion of yourself, to face the fact that you feel you are nothing unless you are attached to a powerful, prestigious man. Is your opinion of yourself inexorably tied to how much money, status, or prestige the man in your life has? Do you feel that you are or would be worthless without a man in your life? Do you believe that you could not really make anything of yourself if you were left to your own devices? To answer yes to any of these questions is not a pleasant revelation, but it is necessary nonetheless. The second step is obvious: you need to learn how to feel good about yourself, to develop other sources of self-esteem aside from your attachment to a man.

Actually, once you stop acting like a Beguiling Delilah, you have made a giant leap toward greater self-esteem. A person with a conscience is bound to feel a sense of guilt if she is exploiting someone for her own purposes. Once you stop exploiting men and treating them like objects, your opinion of yourself is bound to improve.

More important, however, is for you to become involved in activities that will give you an identity all your own. That might mean getting a job or starting a business or giving your time to charity. Whatever it is, it should make you feel good about yourself and should not be related to the man in your life.

"One thing that I tell patients who are like the Beguiling Delilah is to think about things that they enjoy or have enjoyed doing, things that they can do without a man that give them pleasure," psychoanalyst Angela Fox told us. "Almost invariably, the initial response is, 'Well, I enjoy such and such, but I don't really think I do it very well.' If that's true, if she can't think of anything she enjoys that she can do well, it's usually an expression of her resistance to change. But just as often, she's never really worked at becoming competent at the things that she has enjoyed, so naturally she needs experience; she needs to *try*.''

When she does try, the results can be remarkable. For example, Ms. Fox had a patient who said that she loved to draw and would enjoy working as a professional artist. This woman was so insecure in her talent, however, that she procrastinated taking any action for more than a year. Finally, she decided to enroll in one of New York's leading art schools. The last Ms. Fox heard, she was getting all A's in her courses and was at the early stages of developing a flourishing freelance career, and she feels better about herself than she ever has.

One might also guess that she no longer acts like a Beguiling Delilah. By definition, a woman who feels good about herself does not have to look outside herself for her own identity and self-worth. She is free to enjoy a man not for how much he earns or what his status is, but for who he is as a person.

Of course, there is always the possibility that once you feel good about yourself, you may realize that you married the wrong man. If you ask yourself, "What does he mean to me aside from his money and status?" and the answer that pops up is "Not much," it may be time to consider ending the relationship. This will not be easy, particularly if have become accustomed to a lifestyle that you could not afford on your own. As one Beguiling Delilah put it, "Staying with a man you don't really care about is like wearing a leash, but it is a jeweled leash." As difficult as it is to leave, it is even more difficult to live a life without love. Although you will have to struggle, extricating yourself from such a relationship may be the best alternative.

When thinking about the option of leaving, it might help to consider this: if you do not love the man you are with, if he is little more than a money-making machine to you, the chances are good that at some point you will lose him anyway. No one likes being used, and at the point when your Samson discovers that you do not really care, he will begin looking for a woman who does.

For the Conflicted Delilah: Giving Up the Child-Self

The internal struggle of the Conflicted Delilah is very different from that of her Beguiling counterpart. The Beguiling Delilah needs and wants to be taken care of by a man, and she accepts that need within herself. The Conflicted Delilah also feels that she wants to be taken care of, but she despises herself for that desire. The Beguiling Delilah gains self-esteem when she attaches herself to a more powerful man; the Conflicted Delilah often loses it.

Simply put, the Conflicted Delilah is a woman who wants to be taken care of and yet doesn't want to be taken care of at the same time. To a great extent, she is a woman in transition between the old and new female roles but psychologically her conflict usually goes deeper. A large part of the Conflicted Delilah is an adult who wants to take responsibility for her own life; an equally large part of her is a child who feels that she deserves to be pampered if and when she wants to be.

A lot of the child in her comes from the way she was raised as a girl. It is a well-known fact that boys are encouraged to become independent to a much greater degree than girls. The result is that obtaining a true sense of independence as an adult is more difficult for many women than it is for men because they were not taught to be independent early in life. Becoming independent requires a struggle, and although a part of her is willing to engage in that struggle, the child in her resists it. Unconsciously, she may also feel some resentment toward men who, given their upbringing and the social structure, seem to have a much easier time developing autonomy. "He hasn't had to work at becoming independent" is the unspoken message; "therefore, he doesn't deserve to have the same choices as I do."

A Conflicted Delilah may also flit between dependence and independence because she feels guilty about that independence. Many Conflicted Delilahs were raised by mothers who assumed the traditional female role, and mothers often reject daughters who do not follow in their footsteps. This can throw the daughter who does not want to live her life as her mother did into turmoil. She wants to be her own person, but she doesn't want to be rejected by her mother. She wants to be independent, but inside her is the little girl who fears that she will be rejected for that independence. This is why a Conflicted Delilah is often attracted to a man who is a partial Samson. As long as the man in her life stands in the way of her becoming autonomous, she can put the blame for her own conflict on him and avoid the guilt that goes along with not wanting to live her life the way her mother did. The problem, of course, is that although the child in her is secretly grateful when her man does not foster total independence, the adult part of her feels extremely angry and resentful for the same reason.

Another possible source of the Conflicted Delilah's ambivalent feelings about independence is emotional deprivation in childhood. In our discussions with mental health practitioners, we learned that a number of women who are Conflicted Delilahs often did not feel they received adequate nurturing when they were children. Such an experience can have a twofold effect. First, a girl like this needs to develop a high degree of self-sufficiency because she cannot count on anyone else to take care of her. At the same time, she feels deprived of the experience of being taken care of. The result is conflict in adulthood. She is able to take care of herself, but she also wants to be taken care of in the way she never was as a child.

In essence, if you are a Conflicted Delilah, you are a woman whose "child" and "adult" are at war. If you are caught in this struggle, learning to pull harder in favor of the adult is what you will need to do to overcome your conflict. But first, you must have a conscious awareness that you are conflicted. "One of the interesting things about women who fall into the Conflicted Delilah category is that their conflicted feelings are often unconscious," Angela Fox told us. "She may recognize that she has some trouble with being independent, but her tendency is to blame either the man in her life or the male-dominated social structure for her problem. Rarely does she have any idea that her conflicted feelings have anything to do with her early relationship with her mother."

Assessing the root of your conflict, therefore, is the first step toward overcoming it. The following questions may be helpful in making that assessment: To what extent does your mother reject you for being independent? To what extent do you feel that you should not have to struggle to be independent? To what extent are you looking to the man in your life to make up for a feeling of not being loved as a child?

The second step in overcoming your conflict is acknowledging the ways that your conflict translates into your relationship with men. Do you vigorously assert your independence while resenting a man for not taking care of you? If a man gave up some of his power, would you reject him for not being more powerful than you are? Do you complain about a man's lack of emotional expressiveness but find you are repelled when he is "overly" emotional? Owning up to the ways that you really do not want a man to change, despite what you say, will give you a clue to just how deep your conflict goes. It will also help you take the blame off of him and direct it to where it rightly belongs.

Once you have taken responsibility for your conflict, you can begin working on your own growth and development. One way of doing this is to recognize the "child" in yourself every time she appears and refuse to act on her childlike wishes. Every time your conflict expresses itself, say to yourself, "That is my child-self that is feeling that way. I acknowledge her, but I will not let her dictate my life." Eliminate all childlike thoughts such as "I deserve to have things both ways" from your thinking. Fight off your desire to be taken care of with all of your inner strength. Most of all, refuse to accommodate a man who plays on that desire.

Giving up your child-self will not be easy at first, but you will find that each step you take toward becoming independent will be much less difficult. Soon you will want to take control of more and more of your life. As a Conflicted Delilah, you may be part child, but deep down you like yourself least when you give in to that child. Similarly, you will like yourself more and more as you move in the direction of giving that child up.

For the Contemptuous Delilah: A Better Outlet for Anger

Of all the Delilahs, the source of the Contemptuous Delilah's belittling behavior is the least hidden. As unappealing as a Contemptuous Delilah might be, her anger toward men is usually justified: women who become Contemptuous Delilahs almost always have been controlled or exploited by men or believe that men are inferior.

Many of the contemptuous Delilahs we spoke to were home-makers whose husbands did not respect their contribution to the household. These were women who wanted to be significant in their husbands' lives but who found that rather than being viewed as important, they were demeaned or even ridiculed. Their husbands were arrogant to them and did not respect them. Homemaking and childrearing were seen as relatively unimportant by their husbands and were unappreciated. "Whenever I ask my husband to help out with the kids, he says, 'I've spent the last eight hours working my buns off. What did *you* do today?' " one woman told us. "And you want to know why I put him down?" Believing that marriage was life's ultimate goal, a woman like this devotes herself to making her spouse comfortable, only to find that she is viewed as a second-rate, second-class citizen. It is not hard to imagine why we found that some of the most contemptuous women are full-time mothers and homemakers.

Other women had been patronized and used by men in other shabby ways. Many Contemptuous Delilahs, we discovered, were women whose husbands had divorced them after years of marriage. Marian Dobson had been urged by her mate to temporarily give up her career as an advertising executive to raise her family. Nine years and three children later, her husband, seemingly without warning, announced that he wanted a divorce. "You aren't the vibrant, exciting woman I married," he told her. After the separation, Marian met other women who had had similar experiences. "The collective sentiment of our group is that men are immature, selfish bastards," she told us. "My whole life these days revolves around my women friends. I simply have no use for men."

Still others, some married, some single, felt contempt for men because their experience told them that men put obstacles in the way of their independence. Some were married to Samsons who sabotaged their careers. Others had consistently encountered sabotaging Samsons on the job. Either way, many of these women, once they had achieved positions of power, developed the desire for revenge. "During the years that I worked in the corporate world, the men I came across were not very supportive of me," one thirty-eight-year-old securities analyst said. "Some were downright hostile. Now that I have my own company, I only hire women. That is, except for secretaries." She chuckled. "I have to admit that I get a kick out of the role reversal, you know, having women on the top and men on the bottom. I guess I want to give men a taste of their own medicine. That sounds terrible, doesn't it?"

It does, but it also seems understandable. That is the dilemma the Contemptuous Delilah faces: just as the desire for revenge is linked to oppression, a woman's desire to belittle men is more often than not a direct offshoot of having been belittled by men. Given the legitimacy of her anger, what can the Contemptuous Delilah do to get past it?

We believe that the first step is to eliminate all the anger that is not justified. If you are a Contemptuous Delilah who is living with a Samson, your feelings of oppression and the urge for vindication that results are very real. At the same time, there is a good possibility that some of your rage toward the man in your life is really anger at yourself for staying with that man. If that is the case, you might be directing some of your anger toward the wrong target.

Then there is the possibility that some of your anger stems from your childhood. Many Contemptuous Delilahs had a subservient mother and a domineering father. From an early age, women like these wanted to be as different from their oppressed mothers as possible. At the same time, they did not find a supportive role model in their fathers. Dad was viewed as the enemy, and their feelings of anger and rage toward their fathers translated into a generalized desire to get back at men later on. Therefore, it is important that you consider the possibility that some of your anger toward the whole of their male gender may really be unresolved anger toward your parents.

Even if, after self-examination, you feel that your anger is deserved and not misdirected, you are going to have to find a more constructive way to vent that anger. As long as you are contemptuous of and belittling toward men, you will have no chance to help them. We may laugh when the secretaries in the movie 9 to 5 get pleasure out of giving their boss a taste of his own medicine. But in truth, giving men the impression that women want to watch men squirm is no laughing matter, because that kind of attitude only legitimizes and exacerbates men's fears.

How, then, do you let go of your wrath?

Avoiding the tendency to overgeneralize is a good start. In their book *The Intimate Enemy*,[5] Drs. George Bach and Peter Wyden discuss how referring to an intimate as part of a group, in this case, "men," is alienating and obstructive to resolving differences: for example, telling your husband/lover/friend that he's "rigid and uptight, but then again, what else would you expect from a *man*." If you are angry at a man for a particular behavior, tell him. But it is a mistake to generalize that behavior to the whole male sex. For one thing, not all men are Samsons. More important, these generalizations do nothing but breed hostility.

It also helps if you can separate your anger about a specific behavior from your feelings about the man as a whole. Be angry at the *behavior*, not at the *man*. Tell him that he has done something that makes you unhappy. In this way, you can express displeasure without generalizing to the man as a whole.

Understanding these principles can help you deal with your anger toward the Samson in your life. Undoubtedly, he is behaving in certain ways that make you legitimately angry. Although some recent books recommend that anger be squelched, we believe that's a bad idea if your anger is rationally based. Anger that is left to simmer eventually results in a boiling rage.[6] Telling a Samson about behaviors that anger you is different from harboring a continuous, underground resentment toward the man in your life or toward men in general. If you bother to look, chances are you'll find a lot of positive traits mixed in with the negative ones. Focus on them; they will be your lifeline.

Another way of venting your anger more constructively is to put it to good use. The recent changes in women's status in society have been accomplished by women who have targeted their discontent toward effecting change. They have put their anger to work. That certainly beats pointing the finger at men and then sitting back and waiting for change to come about.

Finally, you must ask yourself whether, somewhere along the way, you may have integrated the message that women are inferior. Just as men's desire to control women comes from their innate feelings of inferiority, you too may be covering up your underlying feelings of inferiority by dominating or demeaning men.

For example, many women who claim to resent the superior

status that men have in society nevertheless find that in mixed company they gravitate toward men because "the things women talk about are meaningless and trivial." Other women who express outrage at practices that discriminate against women at the workplace want to work only for male bosses because "women make lousy managers." Still others who espouse egalitarian ideals secretly want their first child to be a boy. To the extent that any of these sentiments reflect your own, you have bought the idea that women indeed are inferior to men. And chances are that your need to put men in their place is largely your way of compensating for your own feelings of inadequacy in relation to them.

If you suspect that this is true for you, then it is important that you begin to develop a positive image of yourself. This might be difficult, given the longstanding message that women are inferior, but it is nevertheless critical. As long as you feel inadequate or inferior, you will continue to demean and manipulate men out of your own insecurity. A woman who is secure in her own sense of independence has little desire to control or demean men. In other words, you need to strive for that "healthy superiority" that aims at being all we can be as people and that benefits everyone.

A Word of Caution

Although overcoming your Delilah attitudes is a prerequisite for helping a man overcome his fears, it is not a guarantee of success. You may completely rid yourself of all your Delilah traits and still find the man in your life unwilling to change. When that is the case, your initial inclination will be to feel angry and frustrated. It may seem as if you have done a lot of work for nothing. We urge you not to give in to these feelings. First of all, personal growth is always to a person's advantage. Second, although getting rid of your Delilah-like characteristics (plus using the techniques described in the following chapters) may not result in changing the man you are with, once you are no longer a Delilah you will have the option of looking for a man who is not a Samson, a man who would not have loved you if you had not given up Delilah.

Chapter 10
The TLC's of Change

Now that you've identified your Delilah traits and purged yourself of them, you are no longer giving the man in your life a concrete reason to fear you. You have taken the first step toward creating the free-of-fear environment that will enable the man to change. As we've mentioned before, a Samson's defenses against his fear are strong, and eradicating both the defenses and the fear can be a long, painful process for both of you. You *can* help your Samson to change, but you must keep several considerations in mind.

All too often we found that women who genuinely want to help men short-circuit their own efforts by having unrealistic expectations of them and about the process of change itself. Rather than looking at the situation realistically, they had an imaginary vision of the way things should or shouldn't be, and then they inevitably felt angry and disappointed when things didn't work out that way. As a result, many of them gave up trying altogether. Others were so caught up in the anger of being let down that their hostility often made things worse.

Many women become victims of their own unrealistic expectations about men, both dooming themselves to disappointment and squelching the potential for positive change. This raises an important question: Exactly what is reasonable for women to expect?

While there are no sure answers because each man and woman is different, there are three things you can probably count on. We call these basic tenets the TLC's of change. They are:

- Expect change to take *time*
- Expect that you will have to take the *lead*
- Expect *conflict*

Below, we have identified each of these basic tenets of change.

Change Takes Time

The most common expectation that is rarely met is that a Samson should be able to overcome his fears overnight. One woman told us that she was becoming increasingly impatient with what she viewed as her boyfriend's condescending attitude toward her, particularly in public. "He doesn't put me down in front of other people anymore," she admitted, "but he doesn't build me up, either. I've been confronting him about this for months, and while things have gotten somewhat better, he isn't where I want him to be, if you know what I mean."

Of course he isn't. How can a few short months undo a lifetime of conditioning, a lifetime of fear?

That's not to say that women should placidly accept a man who is adamant about not changing, who refuses to respond in any way to the fears that permeate his relationships with women. But frequently, women want, even demand, an instantaneous metamorphosis. The message they give is "If you don't change in a week or a month, forget it." Unfortunately, change is very unlikely to come about that quickly.

A woman's frustration when she finds that a Samson usually resists giving up his defenses is certainly understandable, but this do-or-die demand for change tends to come across like a threat. Given the fact that a Samson is afraid to begin with, such an ultimatum will only alarm him even more. "One of the things I absolutely can't deal with in women is their insistence that men undergo this immediate transformation," one college professor told us. "I know a lot of men who think that women should be equal. They're really struggling with their doubts about themselves and their fear of being shown up by women, so they can be more supportive. There are more than a few men who are starting to realize how frightened they are, and who are doing something to work things out in their own heads. But it takes time, and a lot of women don't seem to accept that. One guy I know, for instance, was living with this woman who came home one day and told him he had a month to 'change his sexist ways.' It was like he was writing an article for a newspaper deadline, and if he didn't meet it, he was fired."

What is a man's reaction when he feels the woman he is seeing puts on such intense pressure? "I bail out. I know that as hard as I try, I never will be able to live up to her expectations of me, so what's the use of trying?" His last words, "What's the use of trying?" reflect the consequences of women who push too hard for too much too soon: the man is so overwhelmed by the pressure placed on him to change overnight that he would rather leave the relationship than attempt to do the impossible.

Men's fear of women has existed for thousands of years, and any Samson today has probably been fearful for a long time. And so it is reasonable to expect that eradicating men's fear of women and their resulting need to control them will be a slow, uphill process. A few men are beginning to realize their need to control women for the fear that it is, but most haven't even gotten that far. Within this context, it can almost be guaranteed that even if a man recognizes his fear and the destruction it creates, he will feel some internal resistance to working through it. The woman who expects a Samson to overcome his fear quickly and completely is looking for a pipe dream.

Women should also understand that even when a man changes his outward behavior, inwardly he is likely to be still part Samson and harbor feelings of anger and fear toward women. Many women, for example, have told us that although their spouses or lovers have agreed to do more of what has traditionally been considered "women's work," they do it with a less than enthusiastic attitude. This should be expected. In fact, much social change tends to occur in two steps: first behavioral change, followed by attitudinal change. The more you accept this predictable attitudinal "jet lag" as a normal and necessary part of the process of change, the better you will feel about even the small changes the man in your life is making.

Finally, the speed with which a man is willing to confront his fears and deal with them will depend on the type of man you've chosen. Many women, for instance, are attracted to certain aspects of the economically dominant Samson. Take the famous "why don't you marry a doctor" advice that many mothers hand down to their daughters. Now, there is nothing wrong with marrying a doctor, a lawyer, or a corporation president. But such high-status men are often as afraid, if not more afraid, of women's equality than their lower-status counterparts.[1] It is likely that men like these will change at a considerably slower speed than, say, that of a psychotherapist whose work encourages him to accept and use his "nurturing" side every day.

All told, you can expect to put the superior patience that you have developed as a woman to the test. It helps to keep in mind that the Samson's reaction, basically speaking, is not that of a sexist or chauvinist but of a frightened man. There is little doubt that the women's movement toward equality creates a lot more anxiety for men than for women. It is men who are losing their traditional power. Moreover, the traditional definition of femininity is more flexible than the traditional definition of masculinity. A woman who works has only to expand her definition of femininity to include participation in the labor force. For many men, to accept a woman as an equal without feeling threatened requires that much of his concept of masculinity be overhauled.

Your patience and understanding can make the difference between helping a man work through his fear or making him more afraid. This is no easy task. However, by taking the initiative, you are already one step ahead of the Samson in your life, and it will take some time for him to catch up. You should not be discouraged. On the contrary, approach a Samson with an "Operation Lifetime" kind of attitude, as opposed to a "Change Right Now" chip on your shoulder. Doing so increases the chances that the man in your life will take a good hard look at his fears and make the first changes necessary to overcome those fears.

Taking the Lead

Another pervasive, unrealistic expectation is that a Samson should give a woman permission to break down his defenses. Some women refuse to take any action at all if the man in their life disapproves of, or does not support, her efforts. As one housewife put it, "My husband was so threatened by my working that I feared he would make my life miserable if I got a job. So I did nothing." A woman who tried to develop a freelance career as a graphic artist, but whose husband sabotaged her efforts, told us, "Without Gary's support, the hurdles just seem too overwhelming. So I'm still at my job, but deep down I resent him for not giving me the support I need."

Not only are these women paralyzed by their partners' control, but they also feel cheated because their men are not saying, "Of course, dear, do what you want, I'll support you all the way." What they do not realize is that a person who is afraid is not going be supportive of actions that are likely to exacerbate his fears. And he is certainly not going to initiate them.

In reality, if there is to be any change at all, you will have to initiate it and be prepared to live without male support—at least temporarily. Otherwise, you may wait forever for his permission and his support. Simply put, you have to be willing to take the risk of changing your own life.

The question is, where do you begin?

The first step is to become aware of your own unrealistic expectations of the man or men in your life. If you are like most of the women we met, you have your own set of "irrational" beliefs about the way men should be. Most common and pertinent are the following:

• Men should support equality for women wholeheartedly because it's only fair.

• Since men are the ones with the big problem, *they* should initiate action to solve the problem.

Although it would be very nice if both of these beliefs were valid, they are indeed irrational. True, it may seem only fair that men should support social equality for women. But what group in power has ever given their power away? It may also seem appropriate for men to take direct action in overcoming their fear. But this is not reasonable, considering how well defended most men are. Of course, you can spend your life crying out, "It's not fair, it's not fair," and resenting men for not living up to what you think they should be. In the long run, however, this will do nothing to solve the problem. Chances are, it will only make things worse, and the more quickly you rid yourself of these false beliefs, the better off you will be.

The second step is understanding exactly what it means to initiate change. All too often, and often unconsciously, women assume that initiating change means making demands on men. "I told him that I was tired of the way he was controlling my life and that he'd better change" or "I announced one day that he was going to do the laundry, period" is the way it often comes out. Women who deliver such orders do not realize that they are not taking the lead at all. They are simply passing the buck to men.

While we will discuss the details of taking the lead in the next chapter, at its heart, initiating change means taking positive action yourself. One woman who couldn't deal with the constant phone interruptions of her possessive Samson installed a separate phone line in her den. Another woman married to an economically dominant Samson decided to open her own charge account. Neither demanded that her mate change; neither sat around waiting for his approval. In essence, each was saying, "I am going to take the control out of your hands and put it into mine." And that is precisely what every woman must do.

The initiative approach is better than the demanding approach for two reasons. First, it takes the "I am now going to tell you what you must do" edge out of the situation. Men who are Samsons are already afraid of women. Being told that they "have to— or else" only aggravates their fear and evokes their anger. Second, taking control out of their hands breaks the pattern of men's need to dominate women. For every slavemaster, there must be someone willing to play the slave, and for every man that controls a woman, there is a woman who allows herself to be controlled.

Bear in mind that once you've decided to take the lead, all your problems will not be solved automatically. They may be just beginning. That's because by changing your behavior and becoming more assertive, you shake up and alter the old balance of power in your relationship. Men, for the most part, are going to fear it, resent it, and rebel against it. And that brings us to our third tenet of change.

Expect Conflict

It is here that most women get stuck. They say they want change, yet they expect that change will come easily and without resistance. When it does not, which is almost always the case, they give up, ending up with the same problems and no solutions.

Myra was one such woman. She had entered counseling as a last resort; Eva Margolies was her therapist. Myra's husband Ron had a number of Samson traits, and Myra's frustration had reached her tolerance level. For three sessions, Eva listened to all the things that Ron, or *he*, as she most often referred to him, did or didn't do. *He* wouldn't lift a finger in the house. *He* would only "let" her go out with her friends when *he* had something else to do. *He* would call her at work late in the afternoon to announce that *he* had invited one of his business associates for dinner that night. *He* would always make jokes about "the weaker sex," embarrassing her in front of her friends.

This kind of diatribe is not at all uncommon. Go to any forum where women gather, and you're likely to hear them complaining about the unfair treatment men give women. Expressing their anger has a useful purpose: letting off steam in the presence of sympathetic others can be a constructive safety valve for pent-up feelings of frustration.

But venting that is not followed by action can become a useless and potentially destructive exercise in passing the buck. It is also the direct opposite of taking the lead, which is why, midway through the third session, Eva brought it to a dead halt.

"Given what you've told me, your frustration with your husband is understandable. But what I'm really curious to know is what you intend to do about it?"

"What can I do?" she whined. "Every time I go against what he wants, he gets mad at me."

From the incredulous look on her face, she was totally unprepared for Eva's comment: "So what?"

"What do you mean, 'So what?' I don't like it when he's angry at me. I mean, it just creates a lot of tension and then we end up fighting, and then I end up feeling bad."

"And you're not feeling bad with the way things are now?"

Her body shuddered slightly, after which she paused and nodded her head in slow understanding. "So you're saying I have to decide which is worse, living with the way things are or living with his anger."

Eva agreed, for that is precisely what almost every woman who is with a Samson has to decide. It is not an easy decision. It may very well feel like a "damned if you do, damned if you don't" situation. If you adhere to the status quo, you're mad. If you go against him, he's mad—not just your normal, run-of-the-mill mad, but a kind of "I don't love you anymore" mad, a feeling that is likely to make you feel both insecure and vulnerable. Weighing both sides, you might not be able to determine the best choice for you. But to do nothing guarantees that a Samson will remain a Samson. Unless he is confronted with his fear, he will continue to hide behind the guise of domination, and control the women around him.

This is exactly what had happened to Myra until she entered therapy. Her desire to make changes in her relationship with Ron was genuine, and gradually she began taking action instead of simply bemoaning the way things were.

For example, when Ron did his "guess who's coming to dinner?" routine on her, Myra gently but firmly told him that he could bring home whoever he wanted, but she was not going to cook. The first time, of course, he didn't believe her. At 7 P.M., Ron walked in with two business associates and their wives. "Well, what's for dinner, hon?" he said in that demeaning tone of voice Myra detested.

"I don't know," answered Myra, turning to her guests. "Would you prefer Chinese, Italian, or plain old American? There are good restaurants for each just a mile from here."

Ron kept his cool until they were home again, alone.

"You bitch," he accused. "What the hell was that all about? How could you do that to me?"

"I didn't do anything except exactly what I told you I was going to do," Myra explained. "We had this discussion about a month ago, remember? And remember I told you that I wasn't going to cook for guests anymore without a reasonable notice? Well, I meant it."

Was Ron angry? Boy, was he! In fact, he began humiliating her for two months, and then he went into emotional withdrawal for another two. There were times, Myra said, "when he wouldn't give me the right time of day." Nor did he respond positively to her lead-taking in other areas: he resented that she no longer asked his permission to see her friends; he blew up when she told him she would not go out with him publicly because of his habit of demeaning her specifically and women generally. All in all, "living with Ron was like a living hell for a while."

How long is "a while"? For Myra, it took close to a year for things to "calm down" and another six months before Ron came to understand how destructive his behavior was to his relationship. For others, it takes more or less time, depending on the man and the circumstances. And for all, it is never resolved completely.

"Even after all this time, there is some resentment on Ron's part," Myra said at her last counseling session. "It bothers him that he is no longer king of the castle. I don't think he'll ever completely get over it."

She's right: most men never do. They have too many stereotyped ideas about men's proper roles for them all to be revamped in the course of one lifetime. Living with that fact is the price that women must pay if they really want to help men. But by forcing men to confront their fears as well as their need to be loved, women *are* helping men. They are also helping themselves.

That realization is what actually gets many women through the rough times. Any action that a woman takes that threatens men is likely to precipitate conflict, sometimes to the point of an out-and-out crisis. But once it has passed, usually a new plateau of happiness is reached for both men and women and for the relationship in general. That's because once men can acknowledge how important women are to them, the way that women have always been able to acknowledge how important men are to them, both sides become equally interdependent and equally vulnerable. And that is what true reciprocity, which is the foundation for all healthy relationships, is all about. As Myra's husband Ron put it in a brief note to Eva, "Thanks for helping Myra stand up for herself. It was very unpleasant, and I still sometimes feel a little threatened by how independent she has become, but she's a happier person. And that makes me happier, too, especially because I feel more secure in the knowledge that she *really* loves me." Although it is rare for a man to write such a note, the joy of an egalitarian relationship is not.

Although Myra's story had a happy ending, she experienced great turmoil before eliminating Ron's fear and turning their relationship around. Not all women will experience conflict in their relationships with men, but many will. It is often unavoidable.

What most often can be avoided, however, is the kind of destructive crisis that precipitates male resentment and resistance, the kind of unrelenting tension that often leads to the breakup of a relationship. Keeping the TLC's of change in mind is the first step. Learning to apply the methods presented in the next chapter comes next.

Chapter 11

Confronting Men's Defenses

With a solid understanding of the TLC's of change, you are now ready to take specific action toward changing your Samson. You will need honesty, insight, patience, courage, and determination if you are to succeed. The following sequence of steps can help you reach that goal.

Sizing Up the Situation: The First Step Toward Change

The first step in dealing with a problem is defining the nature of the problem and evaluating the resources you have to deal with it. Similarly, in order to prepare yourself for what lies ahead, you need to honestly evaluate your situation. Outlined below are the questions that are central to that analysis.

Are You Committed to Maintaining a Relationship with the Samson in Your Life? Is There Enough Room in Your Heart to Repair It?

Some women have been living with a Samson for so long and have become so resentful of him that they have run out of patience. There is virtually nothing the man could do, other than become another person overnight, that would mend the scars or ameliorate the anger. Their love is gone.

If the answer to either of the above questions is no, it is time to think about ending the relationship. If you are unable to let go of your anger, you will be unable to establish the kind of environment that is conducive to change.

As a single woman, your recourse is relatively easy. You can simply end the relationship. You will be doing a service both to yourself and to your Samson, however, if you say good-bye as kindly and gracefully as possible. It is bad enough to be rejected; to be rejected cruelly will only exacerbate his fear of other women in the future. We suggest a frank person-to-person conversation during which you give him a chance to vent his hurt and anger. A straightforward approach also gives you the opportunity to tell him exactly what it is about his Samson-like ways that you find difficult to deal with. He may ignore you, of course. But then again, he may listen, take your insights seriously, and begin working on eliminating his fears. Remember, once a Samson does not mean always a Samson.

If you are married, terminating your relationship will obviously be more complicated. Before even broaching the subject with him, it is critical that you plan your escape. The book *Learning to Leave* by Lynette Trier and Richard Peacock will be tremendously helpful.[1] If you suspect your Samson will become violent, or if you no longer feel committed to your relationship but cannot find the psychological strength and understanding to leave, therapeutic assistance is advised.

Is He Interested in Maintaining the Relationship?

Whether he is a super-Samson or a more moderately fearful man, he will be unwilling to work toward change unless he is as committed to the relationship as you are. In fact, one of the motivating forces behind a man who deals with his fear successfully is his desire to keep the woman in his life by his side. If preserving his facade of superiority, his control, takes precedence over preserving your relationship, the prognosis for altering his ways is not very good.

There is no certain way of knowing how committed he is to you. However, imagining a few hypothetical situations can give you a clue. If you told him directly that his controlling ways were making you miserable, would he say, "If you don't like it, leave," and mean it? Do you suspect that he would leave you for another woman whom he could dominate if you no longer allowed him to dominate you? If you ever had more money, prestige, or power than he, do you believe it would be easier for him to leave you than to live with you? If your answer to these questions is "probably not," the chances are excellent that keeping your relationship afloat is his highest priority and that he will be willing to do the work that it takes to do so. A "probably yes" response, on the other hand, may suggest that his need to be the one in charge in a male-female relationship is more compelling than his need to be with you. In this case, you will probably have to live with him as he is, or leave him.

How Frightened Is the Samson in Your Life?

Even if you and your Samson are committed to holding on to your relationship, it is important for you to assess how fearful your Samson is. The strength of his defenses is your strongest clue. The more vigilant his control, the more resistant he will be and the longer it will take for change to come about.

If his Samson score is low, you may be pleasantly surprised at how quickly he is able to overcome his fear. If his score is high, chances are it will take a longer time for him to work through his fear, so be prepared for a tremendous exercise in love and patience.

If his Samson Test score is 9 or above, you should consider seeking professional counseling. If he refuses to come with you, you might want to present him with the "ultimatum" described on page 202. If he still will not move, go alone. A good counselor can give you specific advice and support as well as help you confront certain important questions such as: Why did you choose a man like this to begin with? Why have you allowed yourself to be controlled for so long? What is the possibility that he will ever change?

Do not under any circumstances begin breaking down the defenses of a Samson who you believe might become violent! Stripping the defenses of a man who is prone to violence is a dangerous affair and should not be undertaken without professional advice and counseling.

In sizing up your Samson, it is important that you consider the possibility of his being a closet Samson. A man who does not appear to be a Samson may very well become one when a fear-triggering situation presents itself, as it did for Philip M. in Chapter 7 or Ted Barnes in Chapter 4. If you are a woman who is not employed outside the home or who earns significantly less money than the man in your life, you should try to imagine what would happen if you went to work or began earning more than he. If your hunch is that he would react unfavorably, there is probably a Samson underneath his non-Samson veneer. The voice of intuition is your best ally in making that determination.

Is He Really the Kind of Man You Want?

If you are single, there are a few other factors you should take into consideration when sizing up your Samson. The first is that after marriage, Samson traits tend to get worse, not better. A man often becomes more dependent and more afraid of being engulfed, sexually controlled, and abandoned once he has signed on the dotted line. The fear of inferiority also tends to become exacerbated once a firm commitment has been made. For his girlfriend to be president of the bank is one thing; for his wife to be in that same position is another story altogether. If he is a moderate Samson now, the chances are that he will become a full-fledged Samson later, and you might want to consider looking for a non-Samson.

Also, if the man you have your eye on is a withdrawing Samson, don't delude yourself into believing that you can turn him around and get him to make a commitment. Many women convince themselves that they have the ability to change this kind of man, and although some women are successful, most aren't. If he is a loner; that is, a man who has a history of noncommittal relationships with women, the chances of getting him to make a commitment to you are slim.[2]

You should also keep in mind that if you are chronically attracted to Samson types, you may be a Delilah. If you know a man is a Samson or if you continuously find yourself chasing after one, you need to ask yourself what attracts you to this kind of man. Is it because your primary goal is to be taken care of financially? Emotionally? If this is the case, focus on changing yourself first.

Which Defense Bothers You the Most?

The final step in sizing up your situation is determining specifically what Samson behavior or set of behaviors you most want to see changed. Some men control their fear by using one primary defense, while others use a number of defenses simultaneously. Either way, every defense is associated with numerous controlling behaviors, and you must select the behavior that concerns you the most. You will be engaged in a futile struggle if you want a Samson to stop being possessive, humiliating, and economically dominant all at once. This may be your ultimate goal, but the only way to reach that goal is by dealing with specific Samson behaviors.

If his possessiveness disturbs you the most, begin by making a list of all the behaviors that are symptomatic of that possessiveness. Does he make your life miserable when you go out with your friends? Does he demand your undivided attention whenever you are around? Does he interrogate you about everyone you talk to? After you have looked over the list, zero in on one or two behaviors at the most. Imagine how life would be different if he no longer manifested such behavior. When your fantasizing makes you sigh with relief, you know you've hit the place to start and are ready to begin thinking about the best strategy to get your relationship on the right track.

Planning Your Strategy

As long as you allow a Samson his defenses, he will have virtually no reason to give them up. The question is, what strategy is likely to ensure the best outcome?

There are no clear-cut answers because every Samson is different. However, when considering your strategy, the following points should be kept in mind.

Any Strategy You Consider Must Be One That You Are Willing to Follow Through On

Nothing will undermine a Samson's motivation to change more than informing him that you are prepared to take a certain course of action and then backing down. Your inability to follow through is not only ineffective in changing a Samson's behavior, but it may make his behavior and defense much more intense.

Joyce learned that lesson the hard way. Her husband humiliated her in public, and she told him that the next time he insulted her in front of other people, she was going to go home. Her course of action was a good one. However, when it came to following through,

Joyce backed down. The first time, she forgot her car keys. The second time, she told herself she didn't want to ruin everyone else's evening, and she stayed put while she silently stewed. Not surprisingly, her husband no longer took her seriously and continued to humiliate her. Worse yet, he began putting her down as being a person who was "all talk and no action." Samson has to know you are serious before he seriously considers change.

Slow Desensitization Works Best—When Possible

Many successful therapists use a method referred to as *slow desensitization.*[3] The desensitization process is accomplished by exposing the fearful person to the anxiety-making situation in small, graduated steps. The idea is that the person will have time to adjust to the fear. Once that is accomplished, the fear can be tolerated in increasingly larger quantities.

The same principle applies to many Samsons. If you can strip away his defenses slowly (and at the same time use the positive reinforcement techniques that we will discuss shortly), you are probably better off than if you destroy his defenses in one massive attack. Taking aim at one behavior at a time is a good start. However, if, in planning your strategy, you can take limited action as well, you may be able to defuse his fear without precipitating a crisis.

For example, if you are with a Samson who has maintained economic dominance by discouraging you from working, it might be wiser to break the pattern of dominance by taking a part-time rather than full-time job. One woman we interviewed had been thoroughly convinced that if she went to work, her marriage would be ruined. At the same time, she was anxious and depressed at home. Her initial solution was to take a teaching position at a local college between the hours of nine and one. In that way, she achieved some personal fulfillment without directly confronting her husband's control. When he came home at night, she was as available and attentive as always. The payoff? Her husband, who she had been sure would be furious with her, didn't seem to mind her working at all because by maintaining her interest in him, his fear of not being wanted or needed was reduced. A year later, she increased her working hours; two years later, when offered a full-time position, not only wasn't her husband against it, but he actually supported her efforts.

Another woman resolved a different problem in a similar manner. Her husband was a possessive Samson whose fear of abandonment showed itself particularly when she spent time with her women friends. Because she was afraid of alienating him permanently, she had given in to his possessiveness, never going out with her friends when he was at home. Finally she recognized that he was never going to change and that it was up to her to make the first move. She began making once-a-month dinner dates, and her husband was not agreeable. He tried to make her life miserable every time she went out. This woman did not submit, but neither did she build a greater wall. "I'm sorry that you mind my going out," she said calmly but firmly, "but I find it relaxing, and it makes me feel good. It's something I have to do for myself." Eventually, by doing what she needed to do and setting aside every Friday night just for him, he became less fearful, less possessive.

Slow desensitization works particularly well with the more covert, indirect strategies that you might want to use with a withdrawing Samson. Of course, the slow desensitization technique is not always possible. This is particularly true when dealing with a Samson who is utilizing any of the third-line defenses. In this case, you will have to take stronger, more direct action.

Below are some suggestions about how to deal with various Samson behaviors that include both slow desensitization and harder-hitting tactics. (We say "suggestions" because every Samson is different; there is no simple formula for confronting a man's fears and defenses.) The tactics should not be viewed as hard and fixed rules. At the same time, because they were derived from our observations and discussions with women who have successfully helped men overcome their fears, they serve both as examples of what to do and as assurances that it can be done.

For the Economically Dominant Samson

SAMSON BEHAVIOR: He does not want you to work.
Possible Tactics:

1. Take a part-time job.
2. Go back to school for additional training.
3. Consider starting a small business in your home, such as mail order or child care.

4. Work (for example, typing) on a freelance basis.
5. Take a temporary job during the holidays.
6. Do substitute teaching.

SAMSON BEHAVIOR: He makes the financial decisions because he earns more money.
Possible Tactics:

1. Go to work and set up your own checking account (if you are not already working).
2. Establish your own charge account. (You can do this today even if you are not working.)
3. If he refuses to consult you on financial decisions, don't consult him about reasonable purchases.

SAMSON BEHAVIOR: He believes that because he is working or makes more money than you do, he should not have to do any household chores and/or he does not act as if what you do at home has much redeeming value.
Possible Tactics:

1. Keep a log of the hours you work, both inside and outside the home, find out what it would cost to hire someone to replace you, figure out your wages, and give him the bill.
2. If the above is unsuccessful, stop doing all work that relates to him, such as cooking, laundry, and going to the dry cleaners.

For the Possessive Samson

SAMSON BEHAVIOR: He interrogates you about every move you make or every person you talk to when you are not with him.
Possible Tactics:

1. Tell him all, boring him to death with details.
2. If the above is unsuccessful, tell him that you feel like your privacy is being invaded, and leave the room.

SAMSON BEHAVIOR: He doesn't "let" you have your freedom, or makes your life miserable when you spend time away from him.

Possible Tactics:

1. Set up a night a week as your night to do as you please, and suggest he do the same.
2. Walk away from him when he harasses you, informing him that this kind of behavior makes you want to spend less time with him, not more time.

For the Withdrawing Samson

(Note: The tactics for dealing with a withdrawing Samson are often covert and therefore may not require a direct approach. You also might want to read *Why Can't Men Open Up* by Steven Naifeh and Gregory White Smith for additional suggestions.)

SAMSON BEHAVIOR: He seems more devoted to his work than he is to you.

Possible Tactics:

1. Let him know how lonely you feel.
2. Tell him that you have set aside certain hours for you to spend together, and make him stick to them.
3. Become involved with his work as much as possible.
4. If the above get no response, tell him that your relationship is on the line.

SAMSON BEHAVIOR: He has difficulty expressing his feelings and vulnerabilities.

Possible Tactics:

1. Share a real secret with him; not something you want to let him know, but something you don't want to let him know.
2. Every time he *is* expressive, let him know that you think more, not less, of him as a man.
3. Mention your admiration for men who are emotionally open.
4. Let him know that you need to be closer, offering specific suggestions about ways you would like to see him open up.
5. Set a good example by expressing your own feelings openly and honestly.

SAMSON BEHAVIOR: He pulls away after times of closeness.
Possible Tactics:

1. Give him a reasonable amount of space.
2. When he comes around, let him know that you find him most appealing when you feel close to him.

For the Physically Violent Samson

SAMSON BEHAVIOR: He has fits of rage.
Possible Tactics:

1. If his anger is directed toward objects, put all the things that are particularly valuable to you in a safe place so he cannot get at them.
2. If he destroys something, let him know that you expect him to replace it. If he refuses, replace it yourself, whatever the cost.
3. Inform him in no uncertain terms that if he ever hurts you or threatens to hurt you, you are going to leave him. Be prepared to follow through.

For the Humiliating Samson

SAMSON BEHAVIOR: He puts you down, privately or publicly.
Possible Tactics:

1. Let him know that you are going to walk away from him every time he humiliates you. On the rare occasions when you cannot leave, inform him that you will have no option but to publicly defend yourself by contesting his remarks.
2. Stop going out with him publicly until he promises not to humiliate you.
3. Tell him that he is wasting his time when he puts you down, that you do not buy his opinion of you.

SAMSON BEHAVIOR: He puts women down as a group.
Possible Tactics:

1. Without getting angry, quietly let him know that you disagree with his opinion and why.
2. Give him this book to read.

3. If he does not budge on his opinion, walk away every time he expresses it.

For the Sabotaging Samson

SAMSON BEHAVIOR: When you are most pressured on the job, he becomes excessively needy emotionally.
Possible Tactics:

1. Point out that he seems to become most needy when you need the most support. Then tell him that if he cannot give you support, you will have to look elsewhere.
2. Inform him of your limits, that is, what you can and cannot give him when you are under stress, and stick to those limits.
3. Let him know that you are not going to let his neediness stand in the way of your getting your job done.

SAMSON BEHAVIOR: He makes your life miserable with continual hostility.
Possible Tactics:

1. Let him know that when he is unduly hostile, you are going to ignore him or walk away from him.
2. Let him know that his hostility is pushing you away from him, and follow up by spending less time with him when he is unsupportive.
3. Inform him that his hostility is not going to divert you from the task at hand; it only diverts you from him.

SAMSON BEHAVIOR: He refuses to do his share in running the household.
Possible Tactics:

1. Go on a house strike, doing only what you feel is necessary for yourself and the children.
2. Hire outside help.

The Approach

Now that you've formulated your strategy, you are ready to let your Samson know of your intentions. (If your strategy involves covert action, don't inform him of your intentions because it will ruin the strategy. If he knows what you are trying to do, he is likely to be less receptive to your actions. However, it's still important to let him know the things that he does that disturb you.)

Direct action should never be taken without informing him first. To do otherwise is to add fuel to what already will probably be an inciting situation and to exacerbate his loss of control and his fear.

As the saying goes, "It's not just what you say, but how you say it." One woman with a sabotaging Samson quoted her approach to us. His refusal to help her around the house had built up a lot of resentment within her, but she knew that if she approached him with an arrogant, accusing manner, he would hear only her tone of voice, not her words. Keeping her resentment in check, she first asked him to refrain from commenting until she had finished speaking, and then she spoke to him calmly, rationally and honestly.

"I have been very upset about your unwillingness to do what I feel is your share of the housework. I love you, and I want our relationship to feel good to both of us, but I feel angry and resentful about doing most of the chores when we both work the same number of hours outside the house. It's hard for me to feel good about our relationship when I am feeling so angry. Being in this position is partially my fault because I've done chores that I later felt resentful about. Unless you have any other suggestions, I've decided that I am going to do only my half. I'll take care of my own shopping and laundry, and you can take care of yours. I think I'll feel a lot less resentful toward you. I know you don't like being nagged, and I think this will solve the problem. Of course, if you have any other ideas, I'd be happy to listen."

This woman had constructed a successful approach that integrated all of the critical elements. She also understood the importance of saying everything she had intended to say, despite interruptions from her husband. More specifically, when you approach your Samson it is important to:

Let him know how his Samson-like ways are affecting your feelings toward him. You should never threaten (for the one exception to this, see p. 202 on the "ultimatum"), but you need to inform him of your unhappiness in no uncertain terms.

Let him know that you believe the quality of your relationship is at stake. Equally as important as expressing your discontent is expressing your desire to make your relationship better. Tell him how much you care about him. He may not believe you at this point, claiming that if you loved him you wouldn't be taking the course of action you've suggested, but it is important to let him know anyway.

Be as clear and specific as possible about the action you are going to take, but give him room to negotiate. Before you approach him, you should be clear about your strategy and be willing to follow through. However, on occasion, a Samson might have an alternative strategy that you would consider acceptable. For example, hiring a housekeeper may be acceptable to a woman in the situation cited above, and if her husband came up with such an alternative, she would be wise to consider it. It is always better to come to a negotiated agreement than an imposed one. We should caution you, however, that most Samsons will not be interested in negotiating initially, or their suggestions will be unacceptable. In this case, you will have to tell him that you would still feel resentful toward him if you followed his course of action and that therefore you are going to stick to your own.

Take responsibility for your own contribution to the situation. Remember that he is as much a Samson as you have allowed him to be. Therefore, part of the responsibility for his Samson behavior is yours. Own up to it. Tell him that you know you have on different occasions ignored or submitted to his behavior in the past. If you have submitted because of your own Delilah-like qualities, explain that his dominance had some benefits for you as well.

Let him know how your action can benefit both of you. You have to let him know that you believe that your course of action will make you feel better about him and therefore better about your relationship. Again, he may not accept it at this point, but you must make him aware of this anyway.

Just as you should be sure to include the above components in your approach, you should *never*:

Tell him that his need to control you is a cover-up for his fear. If there is anything that a Samson is going to resist, it's your attempt to analyze his "problem." You are not his therapist, nor should you act like one.

Approach him during a fight or when he's feeling down in the dumps. Wait for a time when he is in a reasonable mood to approach him.

Put the blame on him. This approach only puts an already-defensive Samson more on the defensive. Avoid all phrases such as "It's your fault that" or "If it weren't for you."

Get hooked into an argument when he flies off the handle. Even if your approach is perfect, the chances are that he is going to become angry. Let him vent his anger. Listen to it, and tell him that you understand that he is upset and why he is upset. Then restate your position and create a "time out" for both of you.

Dealing with the Crisis That Results

Now that you've taken the first step in breaking down his defense and thereby confronting him with his fear, what can you expect?

More often than not, his initial response will be to test you: Are you really serious about what you have told him you are going to do? Are you going to stick by that decision even if it means arousing his wrath? Your own determination will make or break the situation, and your ability to follow through is critically important. A Samson, by definition, is going to resist change, and he needs no better excuse for not changing one bit than sensing your wavering and lack of determination to alter the status quo.

Some women get thrown off track at this point because after they carry through on their plan of action, their partners seem to become compliant. For example, one woman named Jan, whose Samson spouse humiliated her and whose plan of action was to leave the house whenever he put her down, told us that her husband seemed to do a total about-face. Jan had arranged to go to a friend's house if necessary, and that's exactly what she did when her husband humiliated her. "I really didn't think that you were serious about walking out," he told her. "I guess I really didn't understand how much my remarks bothered you." For the next three months, his humiliation of her came to a dead halt. However, the next time he put her down, Jan did not walk out. That was a mistake. "He started in all over again," Jan said, "and I was back to square one." Actually, she was not even at square one, because her partner no longer believed she would follow through. The second go-around was therefore that much more difficult. Jan had to leave the house five times over a period of two weeks in order to make her point again.

Ellen, whose live-in boyfriend was a possessive Samson, had a similar experience. Her strategy was to set aside one Saturday every three weeks to spend with her women friends. Contrary to her expectation, not only didn't her boyfriend, Tim, put up a fuss, but when she returned home at the end of the day, he had dinner waiting. Ellen did not suspect that Tim's behavior was aimed at getting her to give up her friends, that it was possessiveness in a more loving form. She made the mistake of trying to reward Tim by spending fewer and fewer Saturdays away from him. For six months, she limited her outings to one every four weeks.

A month later, she approached Tim about going away for the weekend with her friends. Tim exploded. "It made no sense," Ellen said. "I thought his possessiveness was over and done with." What she did not understand was that Tim had read the decrease in time she spent with her friends as backing down from her original stance. Tim's response had been just another ploy to keep her all to himself.

By now, the importance of follow-through should be clear. What happens once your Samson realizes you mean to maintain your stand?

No matter how good your approach or how reasonable your action, almost invariably you will be met with some resistance. In more benign cases, the resistance may take the form of temporary withdrawal or possessiveness. More often, however, a Samson is likely to become hostile and resort to humiliation. He'll put up new defenses and try to make your life miserable.

At this point, your staying power will really be put to the test. Living through a crisis is emotionally trying, but it is almost always the only way to get a Samson to reassess his behavior. There are a number of devices, however, that can help you cope with his reaction and defuse his fear.

Chapter 12

Defusing Men's Fear

To effectively cope with the crisis and defuse his fear, the following techniques should be employed simultaneously. Positive reinforcement, for example, should be used constantly in conjunction with other tactics. The combination of responses will largely determine your success in helping your Samson confront his fear, and it will also make the period of crisis a little more bearable for yourself.

Keep Calm and Ignore What You Can

Your own calm in the face of the crisis is probably the best way to defuse a Samson's reaction. The more you can temporarily ignore his stepped-up defenses (except for violence, which should *never* be tolerated), the better off you are likely to be. When a Samson replaces one defense with another, he is attempting to find another way to control you and keep his fear hidden. However, if you do not allow yourself to be controlled, he will begin getting the message that his strategy is not working.

Some behaviors are relatively easy to cope with. If, for example, you've broken the defense of economic dominance and your Samson withdraws, you should go about your business and give him the space that he needs. If he becomes possessive, you might give him extra reassurance of your love for him.

Other Samson responses are more difficult to tolerate, but remaining calm should still be the keystone. One woman, for instance, found that when she refused to do more than her share of the housework, her husband started leaving his belongings strewn all over the house. Her initial response was outrage: How dare he do such a thing! But she allowed things to pile up so that, within a month, one could not take three steps without walking on an item of clothing. Still, she did not budge. Nor did she demand that her Samson clean up after himself. Her attitude was "If he can live with it this way, so can I." The impasse was broken when her husband's parents announced that they were coming for a visit. "You're not going to let them see this pigpen, are you?" her husband queried. She replied, "Almost everything that is lying around belongs to you, and if you're willing to let them see the house this way, it's all right with me." When she came home the following afternoon, most of his belongings were back in place. He had taken the first step toward real change.

If this sounds too miraculous to be true, consider that when you show a man that you can tolerate a tense situation by keeping calm, you take the ammunition out of his hands, and he discovers that his mechanisms of control do not work.

Appeal to His Rational Side

Another fear-reduction strategy is to appeal to a Samson's rational side. One of the biggest mistakes that women make in trying to get a Samson to change is to appeal to him emotionally. Telling a man to get in touch with his feelings, doubts, and fears only threatens him all the more. Not surprisingly, the typical response is greater resistance. However, to tell a Samson that his behavior works against his own best interests plugs right in to a man's rational side. Since most men pride themselves on being rational, they are a lot more likely to come to the conclusion that their behavior makes no sense.

When Gayle Smith decided to go to night school for her master's degree, against her economically dominant Samson's wishes, he become hostile, yelling at her and putting her down at every opportunity. And he insisted that he would not watch the children the evenings she had her classes. Her first response was to hire a babysitter. She let him know gently but firmly that his refusal to watch the children would not stand in the way of her plans. "If you feel that it is worth the money to pay for the sitter, that is okay with me, although frankly, it doesn't make much sense," she told him. "Not only could we use the money for something we could both enjoy, but I think you're missing out on an opportunity to spend some quiet time alone with the children."

Her response to his hostility and tantrums was similar. "It is obvious that you are angry and unhappy with this situation, and you are showing it. I really don't need your constant anger, but if you feel you have to act this way, then I suppose you have to do it. I'm not happy about it, but I can deal with it. I'm not going to leave you over it." Within three months, his anger began to dissipate. After six months, the babysitter was no longer needed.

Avoid Inciting Behaviors

In defusing a man's fear, it is also important to avoid inciting a Samson even more by lashing out at him. It can be very tempting to retaliate during a crisis, but you will be much better off if you do not. During this stage, you should avoid confronting him with your new plans. If you've gone to work, don't tell him how great your job is. If you've had a wonderful time with your friends, keep it to yourself or find someone else to share your pleasure with. In fact, having a few good friends around to help you get through the crisis is always a good idea because you will have all kinds of feelings, from exhilaration to rage, that are best expressed to them rather than to your Samson. Simply put, don't do anything to stir up his fears.

Reinforce Your Commitment to the Relationship

At the same time that you are holding steadfastly to your position, you also must reaffirm your commitment to making your relationship work. This is crucial. Once a Samson is reassured that his partner does not want to leave him, he is likely to think to himself, "I can either continue doing what I'm doing and create friction in our relationship, or I can try to adapt." Viewing it as his decision gives him a feeling of control, and it is often enough to move him out of the crisis and on to the road to adjustment.

Ultimately, the message you want to convey to a Samson is that there is nothing to fear but fear itself. He needs to know that the less of a Samson he is, the better you feel about your relationship and the less likely you will be to abandon him. He also needs to feel that in your eyes, giving up his defenses makes him not less of a man, but more of one. In short, you must prove to him that his fears are unnecessary. There is no better way to do that than through positive reinforcement.

The Art of Positive Reinforcement

Therapists have long recognized the importance of positive reinforcement in working with patients who are victims of fear.[1] They know that there is no way to get past a fear unless that fear is put into proper perspective. Let's say a person is afraid of flying. With some help, he eventually gets to the point where he is willing to take a short plane ride. If, during his first flight, the plane runs into stormy weather, chances are good that he will retreat back into fear. On the other hand, if his first flight is smooth and pleasant, he will be a lot less fearful of flying the next time.

The same concept applies to a man and his fear of women. If you reject him for giving up his Samson behaviors, he will become even more defensive or leave and end the relationship. But if you can show him that you love him that much more, that your esteem for him is that much higher, his fear will begin to dissipate.

Unfortunately, all too often we found that women had a "Why should I compliment him on every move he makes?" attitude. They take the work their Samsons do to get past their fears as an overdue given, failing to acknowledge the struggle men have gone through along the way. The result? Men tend to feel that their efforts have been unappreciated, that there is no payoff for giving up their defenses.

Patrick Devin was a thirty-one-year-old bachelor who, largely through his girlfriend's prodding, entered therapy to deal with his fear of rejection. He was one of those withdrawing Samsons we discussed in Chapter 6: loving and committed one day, uncaring and frightened the next. The therapy process was slow and painful, but eventually Patrick began making progress. Rather than disappearing for a week, which he had done regularly in the early part of their relationship, he would tell his girlfriend Olivia that he needed a day or two to himself when his fears crept up. Rather than blaming Olivia for placing too many demands on him, he began accepting responsibility for the fact that his fear was his and his alone. What was Olivia's reaction to these changes?

"Nothing," Patrick told us. "Well, not exactly nothing—she did stop nagging me to some extent. But there was never any acknowledgment on her part about the struggle I was going through, about the progress, slow as it was, that I was making." Worse yet, Patrick said, was the fact that rather than compliment him, Olivia continued to complain about the ways he still failed to draw closer to her and offer more emotional security. After a while, he began wondering if all the trouble was worth it.

As he later learned in therapy, it was. Getting past one's fear is always in one's best interest whether those changes are noticed by others or not. But it makes the work easier when a man also gets encouragement from the woman he cares about.

The more you can ignore a Samson's negative behaviors while reinforcing the positive, the faster a man will be likely to overcome his fears. Nor should positive reinforcement come only when the final goal has been achieved, that is, when a man wipes the slate clean of all his Samson behaviors once and for all. If you wait for that moment, you might be waiting forever. More important, if you do not positively reinforce the small changes along the way, the larger changes will probably never come about.

Positive Reinforcement and the Fear of Abandonment

Using positive reinforcement to help defuse his fear of abandonment is relatively easy. All you need to do is show him, over a period of time, that relinquishing his control makes you want to spend more time with him, that you love him a lot more when he is not controlling you than when he is.

While positive reinforcement can be verbal, the best reinforcer is not in what you say but what you do. To tell him that you love him is nice, but defusing his fear through your actions is what will really convince him.

One woman who knew that secret was Debbie. At twenty-four, Debbie's lifelong aspiration to become a concert violist looked as if it might become a reality. There were auditions for a major national orchestra in her area, and Debbie was recommended by one of the orchestra players she had done some freelance work with. Debbie practiced prodigiously for the audition, for the chance not only to be one of the few women in the country to play in an orchestra of such caliber but also for the $40,000-a-year salary that went along with the job. As she prepared for the audition, her husband, Allen, who had always supported her career, started acting like an economically dominant and possessive Samson. "If you take that job, you'll be working all sorts of crazy hours," he told her. "You won't have any time for me. What kind of relationship is that?"

After sizing up the situation, Debbie decided that her best strategy was to continue pursuing the job and to take it if it was offered to her. The slow desensitization approach would not have worked for her because after sixteen years of practicing and hoping for this opportunity, she would have felt too resentful of Allen had she not gone after her dream. Debbie told Allen of her plans, and he almost immediately began sabotaging her, interrupting her practicing incessantly and sneering every time she hit a wrong note. When Debbie started practicing in a locked room upstairs, he withdrew.

It was difficult to reinforce Allen's behavior positively when he was making things so damn impossible. But she seized every opportunity she could. There were evenings that he only interrupted her practicing once or twice, and rather than attack him, she greeted him in bed with an extra warm hug, telling him how much she appreciated the absence of disturbance. Every time they were able to share a pleasant conversation, Debbie made it a point to talk about plans for the future—their future. And when Allen enthusiastically told her that her playing was sounding much better and how proud he was of her, Debbie put down her viola and gave him a warm hug. After a while, Allen started to get the idea: when he was critical and controlling, Debbie pulled away. When he wasn't, she came closer.

By the time Debbie got the job, things were better, although Allen was still not thrilled about the idea. Debbie continued to prove his fear to be groundless. She set aside every Sunday as their day alone together. When she came home after work in the evening, she made a point to spend time alone with Allen. And when Debbie received her first paycheck, she went out and bought theater tickets to a show Allen had wanted to see. "This," she said, handing him the envelope, "is for you."

Today, two years later, Debbie and Allen's relationship is better than it's ever been. They spend more quality time together now than they did before, and Debbie is more in love with Allen than ever. In a recent television interview, Dr. Milton Brothers, husband of Dr. Joyce Brothers, said that "a happy wife makes a happy husband." To that we might add that a happy husband makes a more committed and loving wife.

Support His Masculinity

A special kind of positive reinforcement comes from accepting a man, even lauding him, for his "difference."

As women increasingly adopt more and more traditional male roles, men no longer feel they have outlets to prove their "difference." Women no longer encourage men to have such outlets because they feel, often justifiably, that the ways that men need to prove their difference are ultimately ways that keep women down.

According to anthropologist Margaret Mead, "In every known human society, the male's need for achievement can be recognized. . . . In a great number of societies men's sureness of their sex role is tied up with their right, or ability, to practice some activity that women are not allowed to practice. Their maleness, in fact, has to be underwritten by preventing women from entering some field or performing some feat."[2]

What Dr. Mead is mainly referring to is men's need to achieve in the world of work. But as women are entering traditionally "male" occupations in increasing numbers and are boasting larger paychecks, achievement in the working world is no longer exclusively male. Yet although women's position is understandable, it nevertheless leaves men in a perplexing predicament: if they can't prove their difference in the world of work, where can they prove it? And how can they prove it?

"A man needs a woman who will affirm his masculine power, enjoy it, enhance it and get something from it, rather than envy it and try to destroy it,"[3] says psychiatrist Richard Robertiello, author of *A Man in the Making*. The question is, how can women support men in being men, without contributing to their own servitude?

According to Dr. Robertiello, a good start is for women to accept men's need to be with other men at times. "Men have to go out with the boys. That strengthens their masculinity."[4] If you're saying to yourself, "I already let him do that—doesn't he have that silly Sunday golf game, or that stupid weekly poker game," you've missed the point. You may feel as if you're letting the man in your life spend time with the boys, but if you're seething inside each time he does, the message you are giving off probably sounds more like "You silly, stupid little boy" than "Of course I understand that you want to spend some time doing things without women." Unless your attitude is genuinely accepting, you are not giving him what he needs.

Equally important is to respect a man's need to spend time alone with his son. A number of women we spoke to admitted that they resented the special father-son bond, particularly when a large element of that bond revolved around "masculine" activities such as sports. Often, a mother misinterpreted the normal father-son identification as a training ground for producing a Samson. "It really irks me when my husband and fourteen-year-old son watch sporting events together," one woman admitted. "My husband is an educated man, but when he and Jeremy watch a game together, I can hear him say things like, 'Go man, tackle that sucker.' He never talks that way at other times, so I can't understand why he does it then. And it really drives me nuts when my son imitates his father and talks that way, too. I don't want my son to grow up being a macho type."

What a woman like this fails to realize is that such father-son bonding is not only benign but important in helping a son affirm his sense of masculinity. To teach a boy that women are inferior is destructive, but to teach him that there is something special about the male-to-male bond, that male and female are equal but different, is to give a boy confidence in himself and in his manhood.

After thinking about it, if you conclude that you do indeed resent or disparage a man's need to be alone with other men or with his son, you might try asking yourself a few questions. Are you bothered because you feel excluded? Do you, deep down, think that the way men spend their time together is less constructive than the way women do? Do you fantasize that when men get together, they talk about the women in their lives in less-than-glowing terms?

If your answer to any of these questions is yes, then you can get a glimmer of how men feel about women's relationships and why they are so threatened by them. By accepting your own need to be with women, you will be far more likely to accept his need to be with men.

Another benign way that women can support men's need to be different is by allowing them to use their physical strength for productive purposes. To the detriment of men as well as to themselves, women all too often view men's need to physically assert themselves at best as something they have to tolerate and at worst as a ridiculous exercise in machismo. Many women have told us that the men they know seem to have a compulsive drive to engage in dangerous activities—car or motorcycle racing, mountain climbing, hang gliding. Others say, with revulsion, that they cannot deal with men's barbaric "instinct" to hunt and kill. Still others shake their heads in pitying amazement at the hours that men can spend glued to the television set getting "vicarious thrills watching other men kick around a ball and jump all over each other."

As mysterious as these activities might seem to you, giving men the license to enjoy them may very well be a necessity if men are to hang on to some tenuous sense of masculinity. "It is probable that the young male has a biologically given need to prove himself as a physical individual, and that in the past the hunt and warfare have provided the most common means of such validation," wrote Margaret Mead.[5] Today, most men do not have to kill for their families to eat, and we struggle to avoid war at all costs. That's why it's so important that women encourage men to exercise their physical power in other ways, such as both competitive and non-competitive sports. Such celebrations of "masculine" abilities help men feel good about being men.

Typical male gallantries, agrees author Anne Gottlieb, should be perceived in a similar vein. "When a man opens a door for a woman, he is making a symbolic statement that his superior physical strength will be used to assist and protect, not harm. Apart from their sexual anatomy, greater muscular strength is men's unique human possession. If they are not allowed to use it in a particularly masculine form of nurture, they feel useless, emasculated and vengeful."[6] Allowing men these outlets, says Ms. Gottlieb, may give a man enough pride in his masculinity to ward off his need to prove his superiority in more harmful, destructive ways.

We are not suggesting that you become docile, acquiescent, saccharinely compliant. On the contrary, women should not help men define their masculinity in terms that would force a woman to assume a subservient role. There is nothing wrong with passively allowing a man to light your cigarette. What is destructive, however, is forfeiting your career to satisfy a man's need to feel superior. To deny men harmless expressions of their masculinity is to make them feel even more emasculated and more fearful. But to allow men to prevent women from becoming all that they can in order to enhance their own sense of masculinity hurts not only women, but men as well.

A Little Bit of Empathy

The more you are convinced that the man in your life is either purposely trying to make your lot miserable or just simply doesn't give a damn about your feelings, the more frustrated and vengeful you are bound to feel. Perhaps your best ally in defusing a man's fear is your understanding that his need to keep women down is not a conscious, manipulative plot but a defense against that fear.

Are we suggesting that women act like therapists in relationship to men? Certainly not. Playing therapist is likely to come across as condescending and will perhaps remind him of his mother. What we are saying is that it is important, particularly when dealing with fear, to take a therapeutic approach to the problem, an approach that says "I want to help make things better." If you understand where men are coming from, you are far more likely to overcome the anger that is partially responsible for inhibiting their growth.

The Time to Talk About Leaving

If you have sized up your situation accurately and have put a reasonable plan of action into effect, the chances are good that over time a Samson will change his behavior. The chances are also

good that once you choose a new behavior to work on for yourself, the change will be a lot faster because the groundwork will
have been already laid.

At this point, you should be feeling pretty good about your relationship. However, it is important to always keep in mind that
change takes time and that there will be occasional backsliding.
When this occurs, go back to the defusing-the-fear and positive-
reinforcement techniques discussed earlier.

Some men, however, will not change, no matter what you do;
their defenses may become stronger. There is also the possibility
that rather than adjust, a man might experience a partial or total
breakdown. Even when a man's intentions are good, his fear may
be too ingrained for him to deal with it successfully.

After you have applied the techniques above, if the Samson in
your life does not alter his behavior either because he does not
want to change or cannot, what should you do?

First, you must reevaluate your relationship. If you decide that
it is no longer worth saving, you should make plans for ending it.
If you still want to give the relationship another try, however, your
only hope is to seek professional counseling. A man who responds
to your needs by exerting more control is a man whose fear runs
too deep for you to handle alone.

If he refuses counseling, you have little choice but to hand him
an ultimatum. Firmly and directly, you must inform him that you
find the situation intolerable and that unless he takes action to
change his ways, you will leave him. Sometimes this threat will be
enough to stir him to make the first move toward change. In other
cases, it will not be enough. At this point, the final decision is up
to you. You can leave, or you can live under his control. Remember, for every Samson who controls a woman, there is a woman
who allows herself to be controlled.

Chapter 13

Living Free of Fear: Some Advice for Men

Throughout this book, we have shown how a man's need to control women does not eradicate fear but often creates exactly the kind of woman he fears most. Is there still time for you to change? We hope so. If it is not too late for you, then the question is, where do you begin?

Accepting Fear as Fear

The first step is to acknowledge that your need to feel superior to women and to control them is wrought out of fear. Many men attribute their discomfort with women's equality to recent sex-role changes. As one man told us, "I was raised, however subtly it was implied, to believe that men were supposed to be superior to women, and no one changes overnight." To be sure, the speed with which sex roles have changed is part of the difficulty. But it is largely the fear of women that is the root of resistance to these changes.

Facing fear isn't easy for anyone, and it is particularly difficult for men who have been taught that men are not supposed to be afraid or to make themselves vulnerable in any way. Yet it is impossible to deal with fear, or anything else for that matter, unless it is acknowledged. A good first step is to take the Samson Test that begins on page 30, substituting the word *I* for *he*. Analyzing your score will give you a barometer of both the extent of your fear and the defenses you use to hide it.

Now go back to the test, and for each item that applies to you, add the word *because*. Then write down all the possible reasons for your Samson behavior. For example, if you disparage your mate's opinion, particularly in public, your "Because" list might look something like this:

1. I feel that a woman who expresses her opinion challenges my superiority.
2. I am afraid that she may know more than I do.
3. I am afraid that other men will think that I am a wimp.

Analyzing your Samson responses in this way will give you some insight into the source of your fear. Are you afraid of being sexually controlled? Abandoned? Do you harbor underlying feelings of inferiority to women? The more in touch you can get with your fear, the more likely you will be able to overcome it.

It is also important to read this entire book, not just this chapter. By doing so, you will become more aware of your fears and gain some understanding into their origins.

A Commitment to Overcoming Your Fear

Of course, insight is not enough. Change requires commitment. If the woman in your life has started to rebel against your Samson ways, you have an inbuilt motivation. But although you may change your outward behavior to appease her, real change comes from within and begins with a true desire to change. You must *want* to work through your fear and overcome it.

Having Reasonable Expectations of Yourself

Once you have made a commitment to change, you need to develop reasonable expectations of yourself. Many men, in trying to work through their fears, are much too hard on themselves. They forget that their fears have built up over a long period of time and cannot be wiped out straightaway. True change is an internal process that takes time and requires patience. If your expectations of yourself are too high, you will become extremely frustrated and want to give up before you have given yourself a chance to grow.

You should also expect that your efforts to free yourself from your fear will be met by internal resistance, no matter how committed you are to changing. Altering the status quo, even when it is for the better, is always difficult. It is hard to change old ways even when they are destructive. Although experiencing fear is uncomfortable, your defenses have provided you with a certain sense of security. They also yield other compensations: it feels good to have power, to be the one in charge, to have a wife who defers to you. All of these elements may contribute to your resistance to change. If you are like most men, expect to take one step forward followed by a half step back. Congratulate yourself on your progress, and avoid flagellating yourself when you regress.

Finally, we urge you to put your fear of women into perspective. Your fear is part of you, but it is not all of you. Owning up to your fear and learning to control it rather than letting it control you makes you more, not less, of a man. Fear is a human failure, not a masculine deficiency. To flagellate yourself for your shortcomings is far less productive than using your energy to overcome them.

Getting Past Irrational Fear

Does your fear make sense?

This is the first question you should ask yourself, once you have zeroed in on your fears and have placed change in a reasonable perspective. Although men's fear is real enough, many of its underlying causes are based in irrational thinking. The next step in overcoming your fear is for you to determine which of your fears may be irrational. That is, you need to approach your fear in a more rational way.

A good first step in getting past your fear is to look for the irrational or faulty thoughts and beliefs that may be underlying your fear response and replace those thoughts and beliefs with more rational ones. For example, Mr. Jones's wife receives a promotion, and it occurs to him that she is no longer economically dependent on him. He thinks, "My wife is now economically self-sufficient." He feels afraid that she will no longer need him, that she will abandon him.

What are the irrational beliefs that lead Mr. Jones to feel afraid? Here are some possibilities:

· "If she doesn't need me for money, she will not need me at all."
· "If she becomes economically equal, she will think less of me as a man."
· "If she gets a promotion, her job will mean more to her than I do."

Assuming that Mr. Jones is not dealing with a full-fledged Delilah and that his marriage is sound, all of his beliefs that lead to his fear are irrational. (We will discuss how to deal with a Delilah later.) A wife does not leave her husband simply because she is economically self-sufficient. The remedy for a man like Mr. Jones is to recognize the irrational element in his beliefs and then rethink his position. For example, it is more reasonable for Mr. Jones to think:

· "My wife needs me for *me*, not for financial security."
· "If my wife feels better about herself because of her promotion, she will be a more loving person to be around."
· "The better my wife feels about herself, the less need she will have to prove she is 'superior' to me."
· "We may have less time to spend together because of her promotion, but we'll appreciate the time we do spend together that much more."

Along the same lines, let's say you are having trouble coming to grips with the idea that your boss is a woman.

The event is working for a female; you feel threatened, emasculated, inferior.

Once again, it is not the event that is leading to the fear but an irrational belief that intervenes between what is happening and what you feel. That belief probably sounds something like this: "Anything falling short of superiority to women equals inferiority."

Does this belief make sense? Does equality really mean inferiority? Once you ask yourself these questions, it is not difficult to see the inherent irrationality in this belief.

Thinking about it more rationally, you would be more likely to conclude, "There is nothing unmasculine or inferior about working for a woman." Armed with this more rational belief, the likelihood that you will feel threatened goes way down.

There is no way that we can point out all the areas of irrational thinking that might have contributed to your fear. But there are two general beliefs that we frequently found at the core of many men's fears. The first concerns their relationships with their mothers; the second, their sense of masculinity.

"All Women Are Like My Mother"

A significant part of men's irrational fear of women goes back to their relationships with their mothers. As we explained in Chapter 1, men tend to project both their conscious and unconscious relationships with their mothers onto other women, and because a mother is a powerful figure in a boy's life, a generalized fear of women is often the result.

In order to let go of Mom, it is important to analyze the possible beliefs and feelings you had toward your mother as a child and identify the ways in which those feelings are interfering with your relationships with women now that you are an adult. For example, many men tend to make an unconscious connection between their dependence on their mothers as children and their relationships with women in adulthood. Without knowing it, they think, "My mother had control over me as a child."

Superbelief: "All women are like my mother."

Feeling: "Women are to be feared because, like my mother, they have control over me."

OR

Event: "My mother hurt me emotionally as a child."

Superbelief: "All women are like my mother."

Feeling: "Women are to be feared because they, too, will hurt me."

Breaking this irrational connection between Mom and other women is often as simple as replacing your irrational beliefs about the similarity of your relationship with your mother and your relationships with all other women. Some possible alternate beliefs include:

· The only woman who has "maternal omnipotence" is the mother of a young child.

· Being emotionally dependent on your mother at age four is not the same as being emotionally dependent on a woman at age forty.

· Women are not mothers with new faces.

· Just because Mom had Delilah-like characteristics doesn't mean that all women do.

· Most women want to mother their sons, *not* their men.

· Just because your mother cooked, cleaned, and tended to your every need doesn't mean that other women will or should.

As you begin to understand how you may be displacing your childhood fear of and dependence on your mother onto women in general, you will be able to look at women in a more realistic and less fearful light.

"To Be a Man Means to Control a Woman"

The second superbelief, that real men rule their women with an ironclad grip, is also likely to be playing a significant role in your thinking and hence in your feelings toward women. It is not an easy belief to give up: the message has been pervasive in most societies since the beginning of human history. It has no place in modern society, however.

Men's feeling that masculinity presupposes superiority over women and precludes equality with them is often a direct offshoot of what they learned from their fathers about being male. It is therefore important for you to take a look at your relationship with your dad and the irrational beliefs that may be inherent in that relationship. This will help you move toward a more healthy, integrated notion of masculinity.

If you are like most men, there are numerous concepts that you picked up from your dad that have contributed to your belief that women need to be controlled. These include:

· It's advantageous to be the king of the castle.

· Keeping one's feelings in check is a sign of strength.

· A relationship in which a man is lord and master makes a woman happy.

· A man who allows his wife to work or have a career is only half a man.

· The traditional male role is better (healthier, happier, more fulfilling) than the female role.

· A real male lords over the woman in his life because he is superior.

The fallacy of the last of these beliefs, that is, that men should dominate women because of their innate superiority, is the easiest to identify. If you read Chapter 2, "The Blockades Against Fear," you know that it is only the person who feels frightened and afraid who needs to control and demean others. The man who is secure in himself and his manhood has no such need.

The other concepts are just as irrational and faulty. Being the king of the castle has its advantages, to be sure. But these advantages are far outweighed by the unhappiness of having a spouse who seethes with resentment because of her husband's domination. Invariably this oppression makes a woman want to flee her oppressor or to desire vengeance; both bitter endings are just what a man often fears.

Similarly, the bravado of strength behind which many men hide may give the impression of confidence, but there are great costs associated with maintaining this facade. Considerable research evidence attributes many of the somatic illnesses from which men suffer to their inability to express their feelings. Nor is the traditional masculine role superior to the female role: being the sole financial provider often has a negative effect on men's physical and emotional health.

We are not suggesting that men forsake their manhood. What we are saying is that a lot of the beliefs upon which traditional masculinity has been based are irrational. The antidote? Substitute alternative, more rational beliefs for the old ones.

The list of these irrational beliefs is endless, but you can get a good idea of what they are from Herb Goldberg's wonderful books, *The Hazards of Being Male* and *The New Male*. There is, however, one very rational belief that you can start putting into action right now: Feeling like a "real" man does not come from keeping women in their place but from having a secure sense of self within.

Getting Past Rational Fear

Not all of your fears can be dealt with by applying the rational approach because not all of men's fears are irrational. On the contrary, much of your fear may have a very legitimate basis in reality.

The approach for dealing with rational fear requires identifying the source of the fear and eliminating it.

Taking Control of Your Libido

If you are like many men, you are afraid of being sexually controlled and then betrayed by women. Nor is this a moot fear. The fact is that men need and desire intercourse more than women do, and this discrepancy in need makes men highly vulnerable to the sexual wiles of women. What, then, can you do?

The answer, simply, is to take control of your libido. There is a biological component to men's pressing need for intercourse but for many men there is also a strong psychological component. Getting an attractive woman into bed is, for many men, as pleasurable as a conquest as it is as a sensual, physical experience. Sex for men is frequently a way to prove their masculinity and physical prowess. If a man allows his need to prove himself to get in the way of his judgment, he may find himself getting involved with a woman who will ultimately betray him in some way or other.

"I am a pushover for beautiful women," one young professional man told us. "Even if I know that a woman is not particularly interested in me as a person, I'll pursue her if she's real good-looking. The problem is that then I get hurt when she doesn't want to see me anymore. Still, I can't help it. I guess you could say I am somewhat led around by the balls. It's a macho thing." Actually, it is not really macho at all. A man like this is not in control of his libido but is controlled by it. If you really need to be in control, begin by controlling yourself.

If you relate to the situation of the man cited above, determine how much of your sex life is really a depersonalized experience. All too often, writes psychologist Herb Goldberg, men "are not having sex with someone they are tuned in to and aware of as a person. Rather, they are 'having sex' with a 'thing,' 'making love' to an 'object.' . . . The woman as a person does not really exist. Rather, she is an orifice, a challenge and a proving ground."[1] To the extent that this is true, says Goldberg, sex is not a very satisfying experience, ego boosts aside. And if you are being betrayed in the process, the relationship is probably not very satisfying at all.

The second remedy to your fear is quite simple: you must learn to think before you act. Exercise discretion in your choice of partners. Learn to avoid a woman who you suspect is trying to exploit you. Most importantly, take charge of your own sexuality. Learn to say no to your sexual urges when doing so is in your best interest. Sexual control is within your reach. It is up to you to take it.

Lowering the Risk of Rejection and Abandonment

In our interviews with men who have been abandoned by their wives or lovers, one theme emerged repeatedly: "My wife just got up one day and left. She said she didn't want marriage counseling—we were just through. It came as a total shock." Later in the interview, however, we often heard another story: "Well, I guess I can't say it was a total surprise. It's true that she did express her frustration on a number of occasions. I guess I just didn't take her seriously. I didn't really listen."

He should have. A man who is afraid of being abandoned often intuits that his mate is not very happy with his treatment of her. And he realizes that even if she does not have the financial resources or the courage to leave him, she can emotionally abandon him without ever setting foot outside the front door.

Not surprisingly, the best way a man can reduce the risk of being rejected is to listen to his wife or lover's frustrations. For most men, this is easier to say than to do. Not wanting to confront his partner's unhappiness and its cause, a man may, over a period of time, learn to tune out her frustration. By the time he is ready to really listen to what she has to say, she has become so accustomed to not being heard that she doesn't know where to start. Therefore, it is very important that you let the woman in your life know that you really want to hear her side; that you are ready to listen. It is also a good idea to acknowledge that you might not have been sufficiently attentive in the past and that you are ready to change that situation.

You may also find listening difficult because you may have to confront things that are difficult to hear. One man named Art, for instance, was a sabotaging Samson. After their children reached school age, his wife Maureen returned to her career as a corporate accountant. Art felt threatened and abandoned. His feelings came out in relentless hostility. He refused to talk to Maureen about her work. When she stayed late at the office, he made her life miserable from the minute she walked in the door. Worse yet, he was so preoccupied with his own career ambitions that he didn't notice Maureen's increasing distancing from him for months. Art's first inkling that something was desperately wrong was when Maureen said she received more support from acquaintances than she did from him. By the time Art finally got around to asking Maureen to tell him honestly what was on her mind, she said it in four words: "I want a divorce."

"I was shocked," Art said. "I knew things were amiss, but it never occurred to me that it was that bad." Fortunately, Maureen still loved Art enough to give their relationship another chance. In the months ahead, slowly but steadily, Art was able to understand his own self-defeating behavior better, and he stopped sabotaging his wife's career. Had he not been willing to listen to her, he would have almost certainly been headed for the divorce court.

Of course, listening by itself is not enough. If you truly want to reduce the risk of abandonment, you must make a commitment to work toward a resolution that takes your partner's needs into account. To a large extent, that will mean giving up your dominating ways. Perhaps, like Art, you feel threatened by the thought of your mate's economic independence. Or perhaps you are an emotionally withdrawn Samson who tries to buy off a woman's need for intimacy with material things. Whatever kind of Samson you are, the fastest road to abandonment is to remain as you are. Most women resent being controlled and demeaned. They feel stifled when men do not allow them to grow. They need more than a big house or a new car to make them feel satisfied in their relationships. If you want real security in a relationship, you must view a woman as an equal partner.

How do you stop acting like a Samson? We offer you the same prescription that we offered women who are Delilahs: stop all Samson behaviors immediately. This will be difficult, considering that your natural inclination will probably be to exert more control over the woman in your life, not less, in order to keep her tied to you. However, you should keep one thought in mind: the more you act like a Samson, the more likely you will make the fear of being abandoned become a reality.

If you find that you want to stop being a Samson but are unable to do so, seeking professional counseling can be of help. Counseling is expensive, both in time and money, but it may very well be an essential investment in your future.

Friends: Insurance Against Devastation

Of course, there is always the possibility that your relationship is damaged beyond repair. Even if you are willing to change, if you have been a Samson over an extended period of time, the woman in your life may not want to work on the relationship. When this is the case, and she does leave you, it will be crucial for you to seek outside support, not just in the form of therapeutic assistance but in friendships as well. Indeed, that is good insurance not only for men who have been abandoned but for men generally.

Men suffer more when they are abandoned than women suffer when they are rejected because men are so utterly alone, whereas women usually have close friendships to rely on for strength and comfort. It is poor emotional policy to have no one to depend on besides the one woman in your life. By denying yourself close relationships with children, co-workers, and other male friends, you make yourself highly vulnerable to the devastation of rejection.

"If men put every nickel into one financial investment as they do emotionally with one woman, most would risk being dead broke" is how one financial analyst we spoke with put it. "Most men know the importance of diversifying their assets. They know it is critical to prepare for their future and to have contingency plans. If men ran their emotional lives the way they run their economic lives, they would be a lot better off."

Getting Past Feelings of Inferiority

If, after working through your irrational fear of inferiority, you still have a feeling of low self-esteem in relation to women, you must ask yourself, "why don't I feel good about myself? Why don't I feel secure within myself?"

Although there are many men who are Samsons, there are many others who were raised in similar environments who are not. Why? "There is no way to know for certain," psychoanalyst Angela Fox told us. "It's like asking why certain people become neurotic while others whose histories are similar do not." What is certain, says

Ms. Fox, is that a man who is afraid that he is inferior to women does not have very high self-esteem. "A person who is basically self-confident does not worry that he is inferior to others," she says. "It is only the person who is not secure who concerns himself with issues of who is superior and who is inferior." Your goal, then, is to determine what it is about you that makes you feel inferior. At the very least, this will require some soul searching. You could probably benefit greatly, however, from short-term psychotherapy. A good therapist can help you target areas in which you feel deficient and explore the reasons you feel that way about yourself. In addition, the therapist can suggest ways in which you can improve your image of yourself, both in your own eyes and in the eyes of others.

Remember, too, that it is impossible to be superior to anyone, including women, in *every* way. Indeed, if men feel inferior to women, it is because in some ways they are. Some of these imbalances cannot be changed: women's ability to bear children, or their X chromosome, which gives them extra resistance against disease, are as much "givens" as the fact that men tend to be physically larger and more muscular. However, many of women's "superior" attributes are a product of socialization, which means they can be learned. You may never be able to bear a child, but you certainly can learn to nurture one and reap the rewards of that care. You can also avoid the pitfalls of overwork and overkill arising from your need to prove your superiority, which make you more susceptible to disease and stress. A man may have been trained to compete relentlessly, but you can, and many men do, learn a more cooperative approach, once you realize that cooperation usually works better than competition. If you truly believe that women are superior, you can learn to integrate the "feminine" into your life, just as women have integrated the "masculine" into theirs. As a result, you will have little reason to feel inferior to women, for, indeed, you will not be.

Reducing the Risk That Women Will Use Their Power to Lord Over Men

The risk of being subjugated by women will also be greatly lowered once you get past your feelings of inferiority and strive to treat women as equals. You should applaud women's successes, because the better women feel about themselves, the less likely they will be to disparage men or feel the need to prove their superiority over them. You should encourage women to become autonomous, because a woman who is sure of herself can develop a relationship with a man that is based on strong interdependence, as opposed to economic or psychological dependence. You should accept women as equals, for it is equality, not superiority, that women truly want.

How to Deal with a Delilah

There is one kind of fear that neither is in your head nor comes from your upbringing: if you are involved with a Delilah, your fear of being done in by her may be quite legitimate.

The test for Delilah that starts on page 147 should give you pretty good clues to the kind of woman you are relating to.

The next step is to reassess whether your Samson behavior is at the root of her Delilah behavior. Is she a Beguiling Delilah because you offer her material rewards in place of emotional intimacy? Is she conflicted because you are conflicted? Is she contemptuous because of your need to control? If any of these is the case, giving up your Samson-like ways will probably be enough for her to give up her Delilah tactics.

What if you are not the cause of her Delilah-like behavior? If the involvement is not intense, you are probably better off ending the relationship. If Delilah happens to be your wife, however, it is a good idea to confront her with your feelings. There is no way for you not to fear a woman if she is giving you every reason to fear her.

A View of the Future

Women are becoming increasingly weary of and angry at the Samsons of this world. Women do not want to lord over men, but they do want to be considered men's equals. As women increasingly become economically independent, they will refuse to become involved with men who do not relate to their needs. They will also become increasingly hostile toward men whom they view as keeping them down. Once in positions of power, they may very well want to retaliate against their Samson oppressors.

Indeed, if men do not get past their fear, if they continue to try to dominate women, the story of modern male-female relationships may end like the original tale of Samson and Delilah: Samson used the last vestige of his strength to push the pillars of the Philistine temples apart. The Philistines were destroyed. But in the process, he destroyed himself as well.

Only by striving for a healthy sense of equality, motivated by the desire to be all that one can be in a relationship that benefits both partners, will we be able to give the Samson and Delilah story a happy ending.

It's up to you and your spouse or lover to write this new ending by creating a relationship free of fear and mistrust—one based instead on care, concern, love, and commitment.

Source Notes

Chapter 1: Men's Hidden Fear

1. Will Durant, *The Age of Faith* (New York: Simon and Schuster, 1950), p. 825.
2. From the libretto of *Samson et Dalila*, the opera by Camille Saint-Saëns, libretto by Ferdinand Limaire, RCA Records, 1974.
3. Karen Horney, *Feminine Psychology* (New York: W. W. Norton & Company, 1967), pp. 133–46.
4. Hoffman Reynolds Hays, *The Dangerous Sex* (New York: G.P. Putnam's Sons, 1964), pp. 16–17.
5. Horney, op. cit., p. 137.
6. These findings are summarized in Joyce Brothers, *What Every Woman Should Know About Men* (New York: Simon and Schuster, 1981), pp. 140–42.
7. For an excellent discussion of male psychosexual development, see Nancy Chodorow, *The Reproduction of Mothering* (Berkeley, Calif.: University of California Press, 1978).
8. Saint-Saëns, op. cit.
9. Brothers, op. cit., p. 233.
10. Martha Baum, "Love, Marriage and the Division of Labor," *Sociological Inquiry* 41 (1971), pp. 107–17.
11. Walter R. Grove, "The Relationship Between Sex Roles, Marital Stress and Mental Illness," *Social Forces* (September 1972), pp. 34–44.
12. U.S. Department of Health, Education and Welfare, "Increase in Divorces," data from *The National Vital Statistics System*, Series 21, 20 (1977), p. 14.
13. Grove, op. cit.
14. Bernard E. Segal, "Suicide in Middle Age," *Sociological Symposium* 3 (Fall 1965).
15. Ashley Montagu, *The Natural Superiority of Women* (New York: Collier Books, 1974), p. 195.
16. Herb Goldberg, *The Hazards of Being Male* (New York: Signet Books, 1977), p. 13.
17. Chodorow, op. cit.

18. Ibid, pp. 191–99.

19. Goldberg, op. cit.

20. Eva Margolies, *The Best of Friends, The Worst of Enemies: Women's Hidden Power Over Women* (New York: Dial/Doubleday, 1985).

21. Quoted in Gail Sheehy, *Pathfinders* (New York: Bantam Books, 1982), p. 212.

22. Saint-Saëns, op. cit.

23. Bureau of the Census, cited in *Statistical Abstracts of the United States* (1985), p. 69.

24. *Los Angeles Times,* February 10, 1974, Part I, p. 4.

25. Montagu, op. cit., pp. 74–90.

26. Bureau of the Census, cited in *Statistical Abstracts of the United States* (1985), p. 75.

27. Brothers, op. cit., pp. 25–6.

28. Montagu, op. cit., p. 61, pp. 103–39.

29. Ibid., pp. 142–50.

30. Karen Horney, *The Neurotic Personality of Our Time* (New York: W. W. Norton & Company, 1964), p. 149.

31. Chodorow, op. cit., p. 182.

Chapter 2: The Blockade Against Fear

1. Montagu, op. cit., p. 10.

2. For an excellent summary of Alfred Adler's thesis on superiority and inferiority, see Heinz L. Ansbacher and Rowena R. Ansbacher, eds., *Superiority and Social Interest* (Evanston, Illinois: Northwestern University Press, 1964).

Chapter 4: The First Line of Defense: Economic Dominance

1. Marilyn French, *Beyond Power: On Women, Men, and Morals* (New York: Summit Books, 1985), p. 535.

2. Wolfgang Lederer, *The Dread of Women* (New York: Grune & Stratton, 1968), pp. 279, 281.

3. Philip Blumstein and Pepper Schwartz, *American Couples* (New York: William Morrow and Company, 1983), pp. 118–20.

4. Ibid. This finding appears in many forms throughout this volume.

5. Karen Horney, *Neurotic Personality*, p. 149.

6. Ibid., p. 42.

7. Chodorow, op. cit., p. 201.

8. Karen Horney, *Feminine Psychology*, pp. 133–46.

Chapter 5: The Second-Line Defenses: Possessiveness

1. Horney, *Neurotic Personality*, p. 111.

2. Margolies, op. cit.

3. Robert Bell, "Female and Male Friendship Patterns" (paper presented at Sociological Association of Australia and New Zealand, University of Waikato, Hamilton, New Zealand, 1975).
4. Robert Bell, *Worlds of Friendship* (Beverly Hills, Calif.: Sage Publications, 1981), p. 125.
5. French, op. cit., pp. 87–88.
6. For a detailed discussion of the need for unconditional love, see Horney, *Neurotic Personality,* pp. 112–13.
7. Andras Angyal, *Neurosis and Treatment: A Holistic Theory* (New York: John Wiley & Sons, 1965).

Chapter 6: The Second-Line Defenses: Withdrawal

1. Horney, *Neurotic Personality,* pp. 84–5.
2. Ibid.
3. Ibid., p. 45.
4. Lillian Breslow Rubin, *Worlds of Pain* (New York: Basic Books, 1976), p. 95.
5. Horney, *Neurotic Personality,* pp. 146–47.
6. Barbara Ehrenreich, "A Feminist's View of the New Man," *The New York Times Magazine,* May 20, 1984.
7. Horney, *Neurotic Personality,* p. 85.
8. This face-saving device was documented in Marcia A. Swanson and Dean Tjosvold, "The Effects of Unequal Competence and Sex on Achievement and Self Presentation," *Sex Roles* 5 (1979), pp. 279–85.
9. Horney, *Neurotic Personality,* p. 143.
10. Ibid.
11. Signe Hammer, *Passionate Attachments* (New York: Rawson Associates, 1982), p. 43.
12. Melanie Klein, "The Importance of Symbol-Formation in the Development of the Ego," *International Journal of Psychoanalysis* (1930), p. 281.
13. Horney, *Neurotic Personality,* p. 168.
14. George W. Goethals, "Symbiosis and the Life Cycle," *British Journal of Medical Psychology* 46 (1973), p. 96.
15. Chodorow, op. cit., p. 198.
16. Horney, *Neurotic Personality,* pp. 103–4.

Chapter 7: The Third-Line Defenses: Physical Violence, Humiliation, Sabotage

1. "Rise in Battered Women Blamed on Poor Economy," *The Washington Post,* January 16, 1983, Section C.
2. Daniel Goleman, "Violence Against Women in Films," *The New York Times,* August 28, 1984, Section C, p. 1.

3. Eric Pace, "Paperback Publishing's Latest Push," *The New York Times*, October 17, 1983, Section 3.

4. Beth Sherman, "A New Recognition of the Realities of 'Date Rape,' " *The New York Times*, October 23, 1985, Section C, p. 1.

5. Diana E.H. Russell, *Rape in Marriage* (New York: Collier Books, 1982), pp. 8–9.

6. Andrew Merton, "Return to Brotherhood," *Ms.* (September 1985), p. 60, 62.

7. Eric Fromm, *The Anatomy of Human Destructiveness* (New York: Fawcett Books, 1973), p. 323.

8. This dynamic of sadism is discussed in David Shapiro, *Autonomy and the Rigid Character* (New York: Basic Books, 1981), p. 103.

9. Quoted in Michael Kramer, "The Prime of Jeane Kirkpatrick," *New York* (May 6, 1985), p. 38.

10. Maryanne Vandervelde, "Corporate Husbands," *The Wall Street Journal*, September 29, 1980, Section 1, p. 1.

11. Statistic from K. Walker and M. Woods, "Time Use: A Measure of Household Production of Family Goods and Services." Washington, D. C.: American Home Economics Association (1976). For a discussion of "role overload" for women, see also J. Pleck, L. Lang, and M. Rustad, "Men's Family Work, Involvement and Satisfaction." Wellesley, Mass.: Wellesley College Center for Research on Women (1980).

12. "Daddy Days: More Employers Offer Paternity Leave But Few Men Leave," *The Wall Street Journal*, Labor Letter, April 21, 1981, Section 1, p. 1.

13. Judith Bardwick, *In Transition* (New York: Holt, Rinehart and Winston, 1977), p. 142.

14. Jayne I. Gackenbach and Stephen M. Auerback, "Empirical Evidence for the Phenomenon of the Well-Meaning Liberal Male," *Journal of Clinical Psychology* 31 (October 1975), pp. 632–35.

Chapter 8: Breakdown: The Blockade Comes Tumbling Down

1. Ruth Moulton, "Some Effects of the New Feminism," *The American Journal of Psychiatry* 134 (1977), pp. 1–6.

2. Bureau of the Census, *Statistical Abstracts of the United States* (1985), p. 79.

3. Daniel Goleman, "As Sex Roles Change, Men Turn to Therapy to Cope with Stress," *The New York Times*, August 21, 1984, Section C, p. 1.

4. Ibid.

5. For the range of reactions to abandonment, see Ellen Halle, "The Abandoned Husband: When Wives Leave," *Psychiatric Opinion* 16 (November/December 1979).

Chapter 9: Recognizing the Delilah in Yourself

1. This "different voice" of women is the theme of Carol Gilligan's *In a Different Voice* (Cambridge: Harvard University Press, 1982).
2. Ibid. See also Hilary M. Lips, *Women, Men and the Psychology of Power* (Englewood Cliffs, New Jersey: Prentice-Hall, 1981), pp. 36–7.
3. Quoted in *People* (December 17, 1979), p. 12.
4. Ann Ulanov and Barry Ulanov, *Cinderella and Her Sisters* (Philadelphia: The Westminster Press, 1983), pp. 49–50.
5. George Bach and Peter Wyden, *The Intimate Enemy* (New York: Avon Books, 1968), pp. 107–8.
6. Ibid., pp. 58–62.

Chapter 10: The TLC's of Change

1. For example, as of 1981, no woman had been appointed a full dean in any of the 122 medical teaching institutions in this country, even though women constitute 25 percent of the medical profession. The strong discrimination against women has led to a tremendous need for a supportive network among female physicians. (Judy Klemesrud, "Women in Medicine Find a Need for Support," *The New York Times,* April 13, 1981, Section B.) Similarly, women account for close to one-third of the legal associates in the nation's largest law firms, but only five percent are partners. (Georgia Dullea, "Women Win the Prize of Law Partnerships," *The New York Times,* February 25, 1985, Section B.)

Chapter 11: Confronting Men's Defenses

1. Lynette Trier and Richard Peacock, *Learning to Leave: A Woman's Guide* (Chicago, Ill.: Contemporary Books, 1982).
2. Steven Naifeh and Gregory White Smith, *Why Can't Men Open Up?: Overcoming Men's Fear of Intimacy* (New York: Clarkson N. Potter, 1984), pp. 146–50.
3. Aaron T. Beck and Gary Emery with Ruth L. Greenberg, *Anxiety Disorders and Phobias* (New York, Basic Books, 1985), pp. 264–6.

Chapter 12: Defusing Men's Fear

1. Beck, Emery, and Greenberg, op. cit., p. 272.
2. Margaret Mead, *Male and Female* (New York: William Morrow and Co., 1949, 1967), pp. 159–60.
3. Quoted in Anne Gottlieb, "What Men Need from Women," *Reader's Digest* (January 1984), p. 146.
4. Ibid., p. 147.

5. Margaret Mead, op. cit.
6. Anne Gottlieb, op. cit., pp. 147–8.

Chapter 13: Living Free of Fear: Some Advice for Men
1. Herb Goldberg, *The New Male* (New York: Signet, 1979), p. 218.

Index